advance praise for

THE TEACHINGS OF SHIRELLE:

"Douglas Green's book is a warm, engaging, deceptively simple tribute to the innate wisdom of his beloved dog. May we all learn from such loveable teachers."
– Dennis Palumbo - screenwriter *My Favorite Year*, author of the *Daniel Rinaldi* mysteries, and licensed psychotherapist

"A touching memoir with a twist about how a rescue puppy showed her human how to look at life from a dog's perspective. During their 12-plus years together, Shirelle imparted such valuable life lessons as how to make friends, trust one's instincts, handle hurt and rejection and, most importantly, how to relish the day and live in constant awe and love (All of which the author learned to share with his clients and on the website *AskShirelle.com*, which is imbued with her beautiful spirit!). The reader will come away from this book realizing that if we all approached life as Shirelle did – full of boundless enthusiasm, unconditional love, and living in the moment without shame – then our world would be a better place."
– Toni Runkle, Co-author *Glitter Girl*, and creator of the mom blog *mammakaze.com*

"Green demonstrates the ways in which one can find spiritual, psychological and emotional growth through unexpected sources, utilizing creativity and imagination. This spiritual journey will touch everyone's heart; and if you, the reader, open yourself up to the teachings of Shirelle… who knows what possibilities that may bring forth!"
–   Pamela Dunne, Ph.D. RDT/BCT, co-author *Narradrama: Integrating Drama Therapy, Narrative, and the Creative Arts*

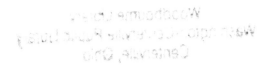

"*The Teachings of Shirelle* is a wonderful story of a truly intimate relationship based on pure love. It takes you through a unique experience of hope, sacrifice, and tough choices. An inspiring book about how a man becomes a stronger and better person when faced with the unexpected joys and sorrows from man's ultimate best friend.

– Kent Toussaint, M.A., L.M.F.T., L.P.C.C., Clinical Director at Teen Therapy Center

"As a life-long cat lover, I opened Douglas Green's memoir/dog bio *The Teachings of Shirelle* with a bit of trepidation. But Green had me at the Introduction. I couldn't stop reading; I didn't want the book to end. When it did, I found myself reading the cover and copyright information, just to make the experience of this beautiful book last longer. It's literate. Moving. Honest. Compelling. Wonderful photos. And now I love both the "divine knucklehead" by the name of Shirelle – AND cats."

– Sylvia Cary, author *It Must Be Five O'Clock Somewhere*

"A beautiful, heartfelt, and entertaining book, that gives the reader a deep understanding of the profound relationship between the human psyche and the souls of other animals with whom we share this planet."

– Linda Buzzell, co-editor *Ecotherapy - Healing with Nature in Mind,* author *How to Make it in Hollywood*

"With humor and candor, Douglas Green delightfully explores the extraordinary relationship between a man and a goofy, irrepressible, and unexpected best friend. His keen observations of Shirelle's remarkable, high-energy life – and the blessings of meeting up with this amazing creature – make this account both inspiring and, at times, laugh out loud funny."

– Jane Hammerslough, author *Dematerializing: Taming the Power of Possessions, The Search for Vile Things, The Home Alone Survival Guide*

"Warm, brilliant, tender and brave - Green and Shirelle teach us that the amazing healing power of love in ALL relationships can last for lifetimes in our hearts... even when they are not physically with us anymore. I love this book and I share it with all my clients!!"
  – Debi Jenkins Frankle, MFT, co-founder Calabasas Counseling and Grief Recovery Center

"I'm not one to gravitate toward dog storybooks. Still, I read *The Teachings of Shirelle* the day of our dog's foot surgery, and am glad I did. Green has dug deep. Shirelle found him and he found her, to be teachers and students for each other. That's a dog, without question. They can be wizards on our path if one dares to cave to the magic and mysticism that they hold for us. Green captures that and more in the book. It explores some deep themes honestly, openly. How we really have come here – to this physical experience – to love and to lose, to experience the height and depths of those experiences to the fullest. He even brings shame – the big human bugaboo – into the most clarified and gentle light. Uplifting, hopeful, real – I will happily sing the praises of *The Teachings of Shirelle* with others."
  – Beth Dolan, host *Being Deliberately;* producer *Regreso, Stranger at Home*

THE TEACHINGS OF SHIRELLE

THE TEACHINGS OF SHIRELLE

Life Lessons from a Divine Knucklehead

By
Douglas Green

Cavalleria Press * Los Angeles

Library of Congress Catalog Card Number 2015908729

For information address:
Cavalleria Press
12304 Santa Monica Boulevard, Suite 327
Los Angeles, CA 90025.
www.CavalleriaPress.com

Quotations courtesy of:
Rebecca © The Walt Disney Company. All Rights Reserved. Used by permission
Sylvia © by A.R. Gurney. All Rights Reserved. Used by permission
"There Are Such Things" written by George Meyer, Stanley Adams, and Abel Baer
© Music Sales Corporation (ASCAP) All Rights Reserved. Used by permission.
"This is Dedicated to the One I Love" © written by Lowman Pauling and Ralph Bass.
All Rights Reserved. Used by permission

All Photographs © 2013 by Douglas Green
except Page 118 © 2005 by Richard Little

First Ask Shirelle Edition April 2015

Manufactured in the United States of America

Green, Douglas
The Teachings of Shirelle: Life Lessons from a Divine Knucklehead

ISBN 978-0-9912281-1-9 Hardcover
978-0-9912281-2-6 Trade Paperback
978-0-9912281-3-3 e-book

Names and identifying characteristics have been changed, and some individuals are composites.

"He painted trees. At least it was one tree."
"You mean he painted the same tree over and over again?"
"Yes. You see, he had a theory, that, if you should find one perfect place or
      person, you should stick to it."
> \- Joan Fontaine and Laurence Olivier in *Rebecca*,
> 1940

Learn about your inner truth from those who know such things,
But don't repeat verbatim what they say.
> \- Jelaluddin Rumi, 13th Century

Introduction

She wasn't the smartest dog who ever lived. She wasn't the nobility Eric Knight or Albert Terhune envisioned. She wasn't a heroic Rin Tin Tin, a sacrificial Yeller, or a clever little Benji. She wasn't even the worst of dogs, a Beethoven or Marley (though she had her moments). She didn't sing Peggy Lee songs or save her ninety-nine pups from a harridan.

She was fast and strong, but not an award-winner. She was beautiful, but not a model for calendars. She was bright, except when she was a total idiot.

But she was what all truly loved dogs are: She was, to someone, the best thing ever.

For her first few years, I thought she was pretty dumb. It would take time for me to realize that she carried a timeless wisdom. And then more to see her as my greatest teacher, a guru of the deeper truths of life. At times I seemed laughable to those around me, as does anyone who truly believes in something, from the Apostles to the Dervishes to Linus in the pumpkin patch. Like them, I have never felt I've mastered the lessons. I was just fortunate enough to be receptive.

In her later life, the teachings deepened, and others began to see as well. And then, as always happens, too soon she was taken away.

This book isn't a biography of her, or a memoir of our time together, though you'll learn a lot about both. This is an attempt to explain, in the simplest terms I can, the lessons I learned, and continue to learn, from her.

The Best Thing Ever.

Shirelle.

Part One:

Knucklehead

Chapter One:
Before

I was born and raised in privileged upper-middle-class society in Kansas City. Unlike nearly all my friends, I had a family unit that breathed stability – with neither of that era's suburban demons of divorce and substance abuse. I was a good student, terrible at sports, and an unfocused ball of repression. I found some outlet in performing arts, with my only notable high school achievements a couple of short plays I directed in an old dining hall.

Most of my free time was spent listening to pop records or watching old movies – entertainments that didn't require athletic ability or confidence – but only decades later would I realize the degree to which I was looking to them with questions I couldn't even phrase yet: How does one become as perfect as Cary Grant? Where does one get Jack Nicholson's coolness? What does Linda Ronstadt want in a man? Why can't the Wolf Man, Quasimodo, Frankenstein's monster, or King Kong be allowed true love?

I had some good friends, but most warmth in my life came from dogs – with the drawback that, until my mid-teens, each one my family took in had been ill-fated: two stolen, and two given away for having attacked people. The last of the latter bit our friendly postman when I was thirteen, a particularly vulnerable age, and the wound of leaving this noble companion incarcerated in an animal shelter, facing near-certain execution, has never healed.

On my insistence, Wolfgang was replaced with a small, neurotic, homely mutt we named Ygor, who seemed to exude a lesson of survival: Don't think much of yourself, and you'll do just fine. A couple of years later, a stray showed up at our door, a beautiful collared collie mix, whom we held for his owner to claim. Since he'd never be ours, I named him "Dog" after Holly Go-Lightly's unowned cat.

About thirteen years later, still unclaimed, Dog had to be put down in my father's arms. Ygor astoundingly lived to be over eighteen – a blind, deaf, incontinent bodhisattva inclined to standing in the middle of rooms with a faraway smile on his face, feeling with his feet in case anyone was approaching who might, not noticing, step on him. He had spent most of his days safe in a recessed window, screaming out horrifically when anyone walked by. Pathetic and annoying, yes, but, in his lifetime, ours was the only house for blocks that wasn't burglarized. Regardless, no one in our family thought he was worth a dime, other than I, who found him heroic and holy. To my parents' credit, however, they kept him all those years, up till the morning they found him expired in the garage. It was that morning that I learned that we don't weep for the dead, but rather for our own loss.

Meanwhile, I had left home for college when Ygor was four, and outside of a couple of summers, never moved back. When I graduated, I followed a girlfriend (and repeated viewings of *The Road Warrior*) to a vacation in Australia, which became a five-year runaway from all I'd known.

Finding bottom-level jobs on movie sets, I dived into joyous temporary communities, becoming a teenager at last in my mid-20s. But after a few years, as I sat at work gazing out at a Whitsunday Island sunset, a voice inside me whispered it was time to move back to the U.S. I applied to film schools in America, and, when accepted by USC, moved, frightened, to Los Angeles.

I had never wanted to live in L.A. – my image of it a cross between Raymond Chandler and *Less Than Zero* – and found film school less of a fit for me than driving trucks through the outback had been, but I adjusted. At one point, feeling the need for a warm and playful environment, I papered an editing suite in photos of Ygor and Dog, gaining some notoriety: "Dude, you gotta check this out, this is weird as $%#!"

Eventually, with little confidence in my skills, I made a thesis film, figuring it would make or break my chances in the business. *Unleashed* was a parody of my childhood world, saying everything I felt I had learned of any worth, particularly in a few years of psychotherapy. The process revealed how much I still needed to learn about directing actors if I wanted to make the sort of stories that interested me. But audiences loved it, and it did get me meetings at big studios. None were interested in anything else I'd written, however, or in hiring me at that time.

I had friendships from film school, but most were falling off as we headed into careers and marriages. I tried to write saleable material, won small jobs writing and editing, and took some acting classes to improve my directing skills, but these couldn't cover up my feelings of emptiness.

I had two goals in my life – a sustainable career as a writer/director, and a successful marriage with kids. And both dreams seemed further away now than when I'd been cleaning out portable toilets in Coober Pedy.

Los Angeles deserves its reputation for a wonderful climate, nine months of the year. Summers, however, can be awful. Inversions hold in air particulates, and the glare and burning heat and smog are lethal and disgusting. This particular September, I developed a cough I couldn't shake. I decided to drive to the mountains a few hours east to give my lungs a break.

Walking through the woods, I felt delirious – my feet on the ground, able to grasp real trees instead of colorless stucco and asphalt. And in the midst of this, I again heard a voice from way deep inside me:

"You need to move out of your apartment. You need to find a small house and get a dog. Because today no one tracks mud into your home."

That was strange, but too specific to ignore. So, while my intention had been to stay in my old flat till I had sold a script, I obeyed. Certainly at this time in my life, I had nothing to lose. Plus, it might be kind of fun to have a puppy all my own.

Chapter Two:
Purchase

There was never a question of where I'd look. Every dog my family and I had bought had been found at a shelter, and any value breeding or papers might confer meant nothing to me. I'd have to steel myself though; I knew the statistics of dogs brought to pounds every day, incarcerated as if they were guilty of some crime (versus the only truths I'd known of them – miraculous giving beings born predisposed to love, protect, and obey even the most undeserving human). And the likelihood for most, that they would leave through the non-public exit.

No one belonged there. Even a "sinner" was just, to my eyes, another unfairly wronged Wolfgang. But I couldn't give them all the freedom they deserved, so I hardened my heart enough to stay focused on the exact qualities I wanted, and avoid thinking about the pain I'd leave behind. After all, I did the same every time I held auditions – though with actors, the ones I didn't pick faced only disappointment, not a lethal needle.

And the being I would now pick would receive, not just a temporary role, but a chance at a life.

*

Friends asked what kind of dog I'd get. I told them I had no idea. "I'm going to walk through a pound, and half the dogs will be old or sick, and break my heart. And forty-nine percent of them will yap at me and run around – like, you know, dogs. And then one will look up and say 'Hello, Doug, I'm glad to see you. I think we should leave now, don't you?'" And I'd know then. Probably male, as I'd always had males.

So one afternoon, a friend and I drove out to see three pounds. The first was sparsely populated, and mostly depressing. One whippet seemed to know what was coming, yowling at me with terrified eyes.

We then went to South Central, so overpopulated that the single-dog cages held up to five each, with note cards listing the inmates' information squeezed between the bars. I wanted to find a young puppy, one that hadn't been alive long enough to have learned fear from abuse. But none here was under three months old. Not thrilled, I plodded down the aisle, my eye scanning the prisoners.

And then...

I hadn't stopped, but I was standing still, in front of a cage. And I hadn't put my hand in, but my finger was being chewed on inside. And I hadn't picked one out, but this puppy and I were looking into each other's eyes. Maybe it was its intense stare that had grabbed me. I don't know. It had just *happened*.

I wasn't sure what breed or sex it was, and there was no information for it. I asked one of the attendants. "Oh. That's Kelly's dog. She took its card. Hey Kelly! Someone wants to buy Knucklehead!"

"Wait, I don't want to buy, I was just asking..."

Kelly, another attendant, walked over and explained that she'd hidden the note card because the puppy's time was up (their influx was so high they had to get rid of dogs after five days), and she didn't want the boss to see the card and put her down. I asked about breed, and they said she seemed to be Husky, maybe mixed with St. Bernard.

In Los Angeles? Wouldn't this heat be a life of torture?

The puppy and I looked at each other. The other puppies in her cage joined in giving me big eyes and whines. In a flash, she turned and bit the ear of the one next to her, and turned right back to me yearningly. I liked that. I had already had the dog whose ear always gets bit. Nothing against Ygor, but I wanted the biter this time.

But St. Bernard? I asked how late they stayed open. No, there wouldn't be time for us to go to the third pound and make it back. What about tomorrow? The pound would be closed for Veteran's Day. And sometimes on holidays the boss would come through to "clean up."

So my leaving could mean curtains for this little thing. But I didn't want to make the wrong decision. I had to go. I left a note saying "Interested Party" for the pup, but felt awful.

We then went to the third pound, where there was an adorable young fellow who looked like Tramp, but I couldn't make up my mind. Frantic, when the place closed, I left empty handed. But as I climbed into my car, I turned to my friend and said, with no doubt, "It's the Husky."

Over the next two nights, I had horrible nightmares, seeing an adult version of this little girl with her forelegs pulled off, and blood everywhere. Very little sleep. Saturday morning, November 12, 1994, we were there before the gate opened. I ran in, and there were scores of younger puppies, exactly what I had originally hoped to find, but they didn't matter, because she was there. I bought her at once, and left a grateful note for Kelly.

This one – too big, too old, too furry, too female – was mine.

*

She showed some independence and attitude from the first. She wasn't as affectionate as some puppies, and was ferociously chewing-fixated, but she was pretty. Mostly orange, with symmetrical white on her face, belly, and legs – and an adorable white tip on her tail. Like my earlier hounds, she had floppy ears, delightfully expressing curiosity, excitement, fear, whatever she had going on. Her large paws stuck out to the side a bit.

She was certainly part Husky. She had their slightly slanted eyes, and the curl in her tail. She also had a Husky trait of pouncing – you'd toss her a toy or a treat and she would approach it and then leap up onto it, forepaws first. But even more, for a dog who would despise them with fury, she seemed part cat, from the leonine way she stalked her prey (often me) – slinky, low to the ground, shoulders and hips rolling her slow progression before the attack – to the kitty-like way she would leave her food out all day, just stopping by for short feedings every few hours.

We went home and she checked the place out, with particular interest in a mirrored door, where she saw her reflection and kept looking around it to find the other dog. She might, I thought, be extremely intelligent.

After a day of play, exhausted, I put her in a crate I'd bought. It was very large, so she could grow into it, but she hated it. All her life she would loathe closed-in spaces, refusing her doghouse except in heaviest rain, and even sleeping under covers only on the coldest of nights. She whined and pawed to get out of the little jail, and I wondered how much sleep either of us was going to get. But then suddenly she lay down, took a large frustrated breath in, gave a loud exhale – and was out cold. Somewhere deep inside her had simply said to check out, that this battle wasn't winnable. This behavior would continue throughout her life – in crates, cars, hospitals.

I was fascinated – I was going to like getting to know this being.

It had begun.

Chapter Three:
The Name

We go through stages in creativity, like everything else. In naming things, for example.

A young child has little logic, and will name things charmingly. My first teddy bear I named "Hi." But my second came around when I was developing a rational brain, so I 'cleverly' named him "Teddy."

Some people's creativity never grows beyond that. Mine probably stunted pretty well there, until I had a girlfriend who had a trove of names she'd picked out over years from words she loved. She named a cat "Gherkin," a car "Asparagus." These were delightful, but did not grow from the object itself.

I wanted to move past that. And, just as I'd known I'd connect with the right dog when I saw it, I wanted to let the puppy's name percolate organically, not from cleverness or a pre-set list.

But others had different ideas. An actress I was working with suggested a French name to match her sophisticated self-image, or at least an aristocratic Russian moniker to go with the pup's Siberian Husky heritage. A friend was inspired by the puppy's pouncing movements to call her "Hoppy." And after three days, the only thing coming from my brain was "Poached Egg," from her orange-and-white coloring (and, I'm sure, some "pooch" inspiration). Not very organic.

(For a moment I considered naming her after her savior, but a dog named Kelly Green just didn't mesh with my style.)

Then I left her for an evening to visit some friends. And on the long drive there, I delighted in how soft her fur was, silky, like chiffon…

Chiffon. Hmm. That's a thought. It sounds like she feels, but there's the margarine brand, and it doesn't take into account her very non-chiffon rough playfulness. But then there's the singing group, The Chiffons. I love them – "One Fine Day," "He's So Fine," "Sweet Talkin' Guy" – they're great. I'd love to give her a name that brings out associations like that.

Like that… Music. That particular music. They call it The Girl Group sound: That bright, friendly, early-'60s, charming, sassy, romantic, funny, eternally youthful… Yes, that's her.

But not Chiffon. What else? Crystal, Shangri-La, Ronnette, Marvellette, Angel, Dixie-Cup? Supreme? Vandella? Shirelle?

Shirelle… that's a magical word. Like Chiffon, it has no hard consonants to match those razor teeth, but it's beautiful. And it's not encumbered by meaning, is it? It has no other point of reference except some great songs – "Will You Love Me Tomorrow," "Dedicated to the One I Love," "Foolish Little Girl," "Mama Said"… This could work.

I looked up The Shirelles in some books, and found that they had invented the name. They wanted to sell themselves as similar to a group called The Chantels, and their lead singer was named Shirley. So, Shirelle. Perfect. A word that means nothing, except melodies, romance, yearning, humor, attitude. Everyone's going to love this name…

The actress was disgusted. "It sounds like a waitress! Why would you smear such a beautiful dog with a classless name?!" I called another friend, and could feel her disappointment. "I was afraid you'd do this. I really thought better of you, Doug." What? "Well, it's obvious. You got her at the pound in South Central, so you gave her a black name. Don't you see how racist that is?"

Whoa! I hadn't begun to think that. Maybe this wasn't a good idea. I didn't want people to dislike my dog on introduction. Perhaps I needed to think further.

Then, that afternoon, my mother phoned from Kansas City, just to check in. She asked how things were going with the new puppy, and I told her the problem. "I mean, I like the name, but…"

"Well, they're right!" she blurted out.

"You too? What's your problem with it?"

"Well, it sounds like a slut! It sounds like some sort of floozy! It sounds like the sort of woman who would marry O.J. Simpson!"

Yes! That's exactly it! This feisty little biter IS a slut and floozy, and would love to marry a big running back with a bad temper: "Come on, OJ, try it again, I'll get ya!"

I dubbed her Shirelle at that instant. And in all the years since, no one ever had a problem with it.

Parents worry so much over their children's names, yet once the kids develop, they define their names themselves.

Shirelle became her. She became Shirelle. And the name developed a new magic, all hers, forever.

Chapter Four:
Social Skills

What are social skills? I remember, as a kid, seeing a book called *Stand Up, Shake Hands, Say 'How Do You Do,'* and fleeing that area of the bookstore, in fear my grandmother would see it and buy it for me for Christmas. As a teenager, trained well in all that horrifying text must have taught, I was shocked at how friendly, how easy in conversation, others seemed to be. What lessons had I missed?

Puppy Shirelle had the social tact of the cartoon Tasmanian Devil. She greeted by jumping on you, biting you, licking to find out what you tasted like, another bite, another jump into the groin, grabbing the cuff of your pants and pulling back to tear it, a jump away as you reach down to stop her, then a lunge at the other ankle, bite, pull, press her paw on your foot for a better yank, run around you, bite again, till you pushed her away and she fell onto the ground, rolling over, and lunging back in for the next bite.

So who was right? Me with my considerate hesitancy, or her with her vile rudeness? I can sure tell you who made friends faster.

Which to her was perfect manners. "As you would have them do unto you."

*

I was constantly continually drying or cleaning her (usually while serenading her with Tom Petty's "Yer So Bad"), and needed some towels that would just be hers. Found two perfect movie tie-ins at a shop. A *Little Mermaid* one, expressing the ebullient rebellion of her running laps for hours in the back yard, and a *Jurassic Park* one adjuring BEWARE! and CHAOS! for this shrew's destruction of a bamboo cover to our yard's chain-link fence, cheekily lapping up the sour apple essence that I had put on it to dissuade her.

The beware that meant, when I passed a picture of an open-mouthed alligator, I shuddered in recognition.

The chaos when a hugely pregnant friend came to visit, wearing the only nice sweater she had that still fit, and the knucklehead greeted her by ripping it on the first jump.

*

I raided bookstores to devour everything I could about her. A couple of books on Huskies listing traits, none of which she developed. A Travel Guide for dog-owners (a bargain at ten times the price). And every training book they had. Most I found heinous – basically how to raise miserable robotic children.

But she'd need more than books, especially an obedience class. I found one through a pet store, and was pleased that the teacher had a no-strike policy, no hitting the dog. The trick was to teach the pup focus, through firmness, consistency, and a bag of cut-up meat in your pocket. Shirelle proved a good student, but so unfocused that lessons needed to be re-taught hundreds of times. Which of course meant lots of treats.

The most urgent issue was her biting and chewing. The answer was simple, if not easy. To fill my house with chew toys, making sure that one is always nearby. So that, when she bites me or chews furniture, I can give her a firm, loud, "No!" and then instantly grab a toy, shove it into her mouth, and congratulate her profusely with rubs, kisses, and excited talk: "What a clever little girl you are, to pick that toy up."

It worked. Long after her puppy chewing was gone, she would greet visitors by running up, sniffing them, maybe jumping on them, giving them a lick, and then running to a toy, biting down on it hard, and shaking the life out of it.

But in the meantime…

*


```
Afternoon. Office in small bungalow.

The phone RINGS.

Man walks into room and picks up receiver.

                    MAN
Hello?

SHIRELLE rushes into room and lunges at him, snapping his
ankles with her gleaming vicious teeth.

                    MAN (Cont'd)
Hello?  Ow!  Stop it!  I'm sorry, hello?  I'm… Ow!  @&$#!
Stop it!  Yes, this is Doug. Who… Ouch!  Sit Down!  SIT!
Excuse me, I have to hold my… Ow!  %#@&!  Don't do that!
I'm sorry, can you repeat… Not the cord!  Do NOT bite
cords!  Ow!  Stop it!  Get out of — Ow!  You stupid… Look!
Chew on this, would you?!

He grabs a chew toy and shoves it into her mouth. She pulls
on it gleefully, till he lets it go.

Push in on:
```

                               *

During this process, I tried to practice tolerance. However, there was one disaster. I'm one of the few people I know who held on to all his LPs after the CD revolution. One day, I put the Beatles' *Abbey Road* record onto the stereo, turned it up loud, and took a shower, singing along with every memorized note. When I stepped out, happily toweling off, there was the cover, in twenty pieces, all over the floor. This irreplaceable treasure, destroyed! Blinded by fury, I grabbed Shirelle by the skin on her spine, ran to the back door, threw it open, and *heaved* her, as hard as I could, across the yard.

Before she hit the ground, the horror hit me: What had I done? Was her leg broken? Her spirit would be ruined; she'd never trust anyone again. Over a stupid old record cover? I ran to check. She was shaken, but she'd landed catlike, with no injury. I begged her forgiveness, hugging her and telling her again and again how sorry I was.

And I went inside and called the teacher's phone number. "Forgive me, for I have sinned."

He listened to my tale of woe, and expressed understanding. And then, "Specifically, did you hit her?"

"No. I threw the daylights out of her, but I didn't hit her."

"Okay, then probably it's all right. Don't do it again, but as long as you're sure she's not injured..."

"Oh, thanks. I was so worried."

"But one thing. I hope you realize, you didn't teach her anything. Throwing her didn't train her not to do that again."

That was his opinion, and that's fine. And I certainly never threw her again.

(But never once did the knucklehead so much as sniff another record cover.)

*

As her behavior gradually improved, her learning process began to fascinate me. She'd do something wrong and get reprimanded for it, do it right and get rewarded for it, and then need to lie down for a nap. She'd sleep intently, anxiously, eyes rolling around beneath their lids, and then wake up having mastered the task. Her brain neurons had visibly knitted during the sleep, figuring out the logic of the lesson. It was beautiful.

So, within a month, she had learned to come, sit, heel, and fetch. She was also perfectly housetrained – almost. There were exceptions, such as the night I arrived home after a degrading reaming from a use-you-as-an-example acting teacher, and she took one look at my face, squatted, and emptied out her anxiety.

*

Each day she grew. And as she grew, a funny thing happened. She seemed to become a mix of Wolfgang, Ygor, and Dog – Wolf's shape, Ygor's expressions, and Dog's coloring. And Wolfgang's brains, Ygor's sweetness, and Dog's self-centeredness. But as much as I esteemed their memories, I had no desire for Shirelle to be like them. I wanted her to be herself. Her own animal.

But if that true self were to emulate anyone, I knew who that should be.

Annie.

Annie was the smartest dog I'd ever met. Her owner had married one of my best friends from film school, and Annie was the high point of his dowry. Playful, loving, silly, but so beautifully trained that if he, in the middle of a conversation, turned and pointed his finger and muttered "Bang!" she would collapse onto her back, and freeze at once. At their wedding, Annie was the ring bearer and led the party (though it required them putting the rings in a basket, with a tennis ball around the handle).

From the day I brought Shirelle home, I wanted them to meet. "This is what a perfect dog is like! See how obedient she is? How focused? But she's still all dog! This, little one, is what we call a role model!"

Annie's owners were ambivalent. "She's really a people dog." "She doesn't get along well with other dogs." "I don't think it's going to work out." But I didn't care about Annie becoming Shirelle's best pal; I just wanted the pup to learn, to pick up what perfection was like.

We went into their back yard. They saw each other. Thrilled at a playmate, Shirelle leapt to her and pounced up with her paws of love. And Annie, sweet loving wonderful Annie, went rabid. Hateful rage blazing, she lunged onto the puppy, teeth diving for the kill. Shirelle screamed out, I jerked her up while Annie's owners yanked her back. She had drawn blood, just above Shirelle's right eye, and none doubted the eye itself would have been ripped out if we'd been slower.

Annie was a people dog. She didn't get along with other dogs. It didn't work out.

In all our future meetings, Annie was just as wonderful to me as ever, and I to her. This wasn't her fault. Shirelle and I both just had to learn a lesson about naively trusting strangers, or even a sweetheart we're sure we know.

*

I was fond of the little brat, sure. But I wasn't in love yet. That fall would come at one particular moment.

She hadn't barked. Some huskies don't, so I wondered if she ever would. I knew it would be a mixed blessing – nice to not have the noise, but Ygor's yowling had sure protected that house.

She squatted and peed on the rug beneath the dining table. I pointed at it, pushed her nose toward it, and sternly said "No."

She started to lick the urine. "No."

She turned to chew on me. "No."

She went back to licking the urine, which I was now covering with a cleaning powder. "No!" Each time sterner and louder than the last.

She turned and started biting the table leg. "*No!*"

She bit my ankle again. "No!"

She started licking up the powder and urine again. "*NO!*"

She whipped her head up and glared into my eyes. Filled with frustration and fury, she opened her mouth. "Rrr-rrr-oh-AOU!" It was her first bark, but you couldn't quite call it a bark. More a growl that became a yelp.

And I melted. Picked her up and kissed her. Of course she was frustrated, fed up. Trying to please, but filled with anxious bite, what was she supposed to do? And this first word, this obscenity, was so heartfelt, so in-my-face, so adorable.

This moment was a gift, one whose importance I wouldn't grasp for years. Infants look for limits, but many parents react by just berating them, which breaks down the child's self-esteem instead of teaching those boundaries. While other parents are afraid to enforce rules at all. Here she was taught the limits, but her voice, her honest expression, was greeted with love and acceptance. How many bad messages do kids get when going through the "terrible twos?" Shirelle got no such words that day. The statement of the lesson – besides please don't pee on the rug – was that she was wonderful, lovable, and deserving.

Eventually she developed an ugly, loud bark. But she never felt bad about it, because she'd learned early on that her voice was loved.

As the song warned, be careful: Children do listen, and learn.

Chapter Five:
Connections

If dogs are so loyal, how does one account for this puppy's knowing disobedience?

Because it wasn't disloyalty. Within the boundaries of our relationship, she wanted to test everything she could, and get away with as much as possible. But she never wanted to leave those boundaries, caring more about making sure I was there for her and doing okay than anything else in her life.

And something was beginning. While she spent most of the time in this hyperactive rebellion, we were getting these moments – seconds of looking into each other's eyes and connecting, "getting" each other. I would flow with new nicknames. Puppy and Pooch led to Pupperooni, Pooper, Pooperhead, Mrs. Poop, endless loving vulgarities.

Still gazing, she to me, I to her. Beautiful calms in the eye of her storm.

*

She was very poor at catching, with lousy eye-mouth coordination. But she loved chasing anything possible – not just to please me, but because it kept the action-filled attention going.

Meanwhile, we invented wonderful games. The best was a tug-of-war, in which she would grab onto the end of a 3-foot rope toy and try to pull my arms out of their sockets, while I would gently pull back (If I jerked her as hard as she jerked me, I might break her teeth). But once the rope was taut, instead of jerking, she would brace her legs fully, and I would drag her across our wood floor, while she held her head low to make sure of the perfect skiing experience. Then I'd kick into gear and spin quickly, and she'd reel around the room. Until the second I relaxed, when the jerking would begin again.

When we needed a breath, rope taut, I would move my face in to where our noses were touching, and growl. She'd follow suit, and we'd jump back into it, pulling, jerking, skiing, swinging, close-up mutually-affectionate growling, again and again.

People saw the game and thought I was torturing the puppy. But I had to store the rope toy out of her reach, because she would insist on it all day.

For her, this was dancing at its best, with its intimacy, embracing, excitement, and exhausting physicality.

*

One giant question in life is how to deal with the unacceptable and unavoidable. Viktor Frankl's famed *Man's Search for Meaning* tells of his experiences in a Nazi prison camp, where he managed to deepen his faith and love for humanity. Luckily, most of us aren't tested to that degree, but tests still exist. What do you do if you have no choice, and what you hate and fear most is happening right now?

Shirelle hated anything where water came onto her from above. Hated sprinklers, hated rain (though if I were walking her, my being there somehow made it tolerable). And most of all, loathed baths. As a puppy, she fought like crazy to get out from them, so I tried multiple alternatives – hose, shower, groomers – but none left her feeling any better. Really, the best way was to stick her in the tub and get it done quickly. She learned to accept it, trembling in misery, knowing there was no choice. For her whole life, any time I ran a tub faucet, she would shake.

Unlike Frankl, Shirelle never found a deep meaning in her hell. What made it okay was that after the bath she got whatever she wanted - lots of kisses and hugs and treats and indulgent play. And of course my accepting it when she shook soapy water all over the room and me. She still dreaded the process, but I made it bearable with overwhelming reward.

Can we do that for ourselves? Spend Thanksgiving with the awful in-laws, but know that when you get home, you'll give yourself a cigar, chocolate, whatever? It's got to help.

And if you're condemned to live in Auschwitz, it's probably a good idea to believe in a heaven.

*

My parents hadn't allowed our dogs in the front part of our house, thereby keeping our bedrooms sterile. My boyhood craving to sleep with Wolfgang or Ygor at my side had never been sated. So, although all the training guides insisted that allowing dogs onto beds causes problems, I very gladly invited Shirelle up as soon as she could last the night outside her crate. At first, she wanted to chew and bite, but slowly she learned that this was sacred time together.

Only two problems transpired. First, why would a dog, even after years of being pushed aside, insist on lying *across* the bed before the person comes to sleep? She can't have enjoyed my shoving; certainly her nightly groan implied she didn't.

(Which suggests the question: in "Lay, Lady, Lay" why does Bob Dylan have her recline "*across* my big brass bed?" Did Sara have this same quirk?)

The other was easily remedied. If she had the run of the house, she'd choose to sleep by the front window. Then when a car, or a pedestrian, or (worst of all) a *cat* happened by at three in the morning, she'd let out an alarm to wake stone. So I learned to fasten the bedroom door, so she couldn't leave through the night.

A routine developed. She would go to bed before me, *across* the bed. Then I'd shove her to one side and climb in next to her. After I fell asleep, maybe an hour would go by before she'd get too warm, and jump off the bed. Then at some point, she'd choose to jump back on, and lay her full weight back against me.

Is there a more comforting feeling than to be in the middle of a dream, and brought to semi-wakefulness by the motion of someone fully adored? A spouse, a baby, Shirelle – all provide this deepest joy.

*

But Shirelle wasn't the only thing messing with my sleep. I was in love. In love with a woman who was involved with another man. And, as the puppy began demanding less of my free time, this secret relationship deepened.

A few years later, the media had a heyday exploiting every detail when a White House intern had a fling with the President. And as I heard or read interviews with Miss Lewinsky, I related so well. The idiocy one has when told that your beloved will leave that other person, "Just give me time." Maybe the teller even believes it, but we should know better. Today, I'm sure Monica does. So do I.

The huge highs when we'd meet, the devastating lows when I'd know she was with him – laughing, embracing, forgetting. And, mired in this drama, the "other one" is so pathetically obsessed that he can't appreciate or even see what's right in front of his eyes.

Shirelle. Sitting in her doghouse in the rain, miserable. Me seeing her through the window, feeling exactly what she felt. But too trapped in my personal asphalt to bring her inside and put up with her biting and wanting to play all the time.

Begging with unheard genius: "Stop thinking about her, you moron! Come on, play tug-of-war, throw something, or just wrestle with me! Life is here! All that's there is dreariness and soul-death!"

*

When the pain got to be too much, I fixed a tarp to protect the car seats from her scratching and shedding, and took her for a weekend to the barren beauty of the Joshua Tree desert, where she climbed rocks with me, scared of the heights but still keeping up. Momentarily free of my other heart-tie, I realized that was what I was looking for – someone who would at least try.

And when the inevitable occurred, when the woman came to realize she was living a lie, that she'd never leave him, and left me instead, I felt as though everything in my life had been ripped out from inside me. And, with Shirelle, I began the process of escaping my memory-resonant home and environs as much as I could.

*

I used the dog travel guide to find a secluded beach a few hours away. Feeling the world peeling off, driving winding roads forever, till we reached a breathtaking shore, where Shirelle nearly pulled my wrist apart in her eagerness to get around. For me, it was the endless horizon, but for her, it was the smells, the smells, the smells! Never had she so resented being tied to me.

It's illegal to have dogs off leash there, but it's cliffy, and after you get around the first cliff, you have no problem with cops or lifeguards. I let her go, and she exploded. Bounding, with legs now extending long, chasing birds, not caring that they were too high up for her to reach, sniffing out tiny crabs, and running into other dogs with such energy and glee that both would roll to the ground from the impact. Some jumping on people too, but not so much – we aren't nearly as fun.

Other times, she'd gallop away, sniffing with passionate zeal until she was maybe fifty or a hundred yards away, and then suddenly run at me with everything she had, ears back, chest almost at the ground, and a huge smile on her face – and then, just as she got to me, swing a fake-out, pass me and shift into a gazelle-like bounce until she found something else to excite her.

There comes a point, where the connection between individuals becomes so intense that one literally has a physical reaction to what the other experiences. So while half the time I was ruminating about my lost life, the other half I was feeling the same release Shirelle was. Or maybe better than hers. That's the best kind of love, where the adored is as happy as possible, but I'm happier at her happiness than she is, a happiness far deeper than I can have for myself.

Relaxing on the sand, I read from *The Call of the Wild*, about her ancestor Buck, rescued by an owner who brought out:

> *"Love, genuine passionate love … love that was feverish and burning, that was adoration, that was madness… content to adore at a distance, looking up into his face, dwelling upon it, studying it, following with keenest interest each fleeting expression, every movement or change of feature…"*

How silly for me to feel unloved, when these words were proven by this magical spirit, right there, lying on her chest, eyes gazing at me?

And so, having escaped out of civilization and into each other's selves, we got home refreshed and exhausted, and very bonded.

And then I gave her a bath and ruined everything. And went right back to my abandoned depression.

*

I lay on the bed, talking talking talking, ruminating, "What did she mean when…? When she did that, I should have said… She's going to change her mind when she… I'm better off because I'm going to…"

And as I got more and more desperate, the tired bored soul lying next to me sat up, took a step over, and placed herself down with a groan, flopping her neck and long chin directly onto my heart. I gasped at the connection, and, at last, burst into sobs.

I'd been trying not to exist, and she'd just argued, "You do, pal."

How did she know to do that? How was she that brilliant?

*

We take more and longer hikes.

She's chasing a bird, looking like Mr. Lunch. Running full speed toward a fence of wire so thin she can't tell it's there, and I can't stop her. The bird pulls upward, and she suddenly sees the fence and slams on her brakes, missing it by an inch.

Shirelle's happy now. Life goes on, she bounces in the water and the river runs.

There's beauty to be found everywhere. People say to me, "You're attracted to the unavailable." But this, so close, is gold.

*

She got spayed on the day of the Oscars, when of course her fella and she would be at a party, laughing, cheering. I visited her in her hospital cell after the operation – desexed, miserable, trapped on cold concrete, aching from the betrayal of abandonment. We were each other.

The next weeks were recovery for both of us. She had to learn that jumping onto or off of the bed really hurt (her landing yelps hurt me just as much – well, no, probably they didn't), and to depend on me coming when she whined, to lift her on or off. And I needed that needing.

*

I had a dream about running to airports to get people to planes. I'd forgotten Shirelle, left her somewhere to do more duties. And I was in the back part of my parents' house, and there Shirelle came, climbing the stairs, finding me.

*

I did see the woman again. She phoned me about six months later, and asked me out for a drink. We poured out our hearts, grateful to reconnect. A few days later, I got another call, her voice filled with hatred. She appeared at my door. Shirelle was overjoyed, ran up to embrace her, and she kicked her down, "Get her *off* of me!" Spouted a half-hour of resentment and accusations. Maybe she believed them, maybe not. But the hate was real.

She left, and I misted to a state I had never known before, shivering, literally freezing. I wasn't angry, or even hurt. She had shamed me to such a degree that I had gone into low-level shock. The only warmth I could find was to hold Shirelle against me and soak up her loving heat.

Later, when she called to apologize, to gently coo lines on my answering machine like, "I know you must hate me, but…," I'd drop everything and run Shirelle out for a long walk, so that if she should drive across town to our home, she'd find us not there.

Eventually, she stopped calling, and that was that. The beautiful memories were now facts in my head, while my body only remembered the chill, not her touch.

I had won. The freezer was gone, and the warmer was still there, appreciated at last.

If you need tablets and booming voices to tell you what not to do, then fine, follow the Ten Commandments or whatever works. But the reason not to cheat isn't because of the hell that awaits after this life; it's the Inferno that's right here.

How irrelevant a woman must feel, to save a stained dress and want to become infamous worldwide for degrading imagery. But it doesn't take a President to make one feel that way.

Nor does it require months of an obnoxious, disobedient, assaultive puppy to pull one out of it – whose patient impatience was forging a bond that could never be broken.

But it sure helps.

Chapter Six:
Snapshots of a Boy and His Dog

Hairs in my living room
Hairs up my nose
Hairs in my car
Hairs in my clothes
Hairs in my cereal
Hairs in my tub
Hairs at the office
Hairs at the pub
Brushfull after Brushfull
Fill a grocery bag
You don't like me brushing?
Don't like to hear me nag?
You want to be left alone
Not suffering this pain?
You'd rather play some tug-of-war?
Then would you please explain
The hairs on my pillow
Hairs north and south

Hairs in my eyelids
And stuck inside my mouth

You know they look just awful
It's strange the way they do –
They always radiate such light
While they're still on you.

*

It's sauna hot in Arizona and Nevada. It's a long way to Colorado, to meet my newborn nephew, but she handles it well. We get to the roadway that leads to their house, and I let her out of the confining car. She chases me joyfully (or is she scared I'm leaving her behind?). I look ahead and see my seven-year-old niece sweetly waiting outside the door for me. Without warning, the orange torpedo with the running start tackles her.

There are predators in the woods nearby, so we tie Shirelle up to a tree with a metal lead. She runs it from one length to the other, having a great time, then jumps so hard she breaks the 1000-pound cable, without even a yelp as her neck snaps it.

My family is impressed, but frightened. What in God's name is this creature?!

*

Our house is in a friendly neighborhood, homey though near giant freeways. The area housed a number of Japanese-Americans before World War II, who were then placed into camps for the duration of the war. Afterward, the government in its guilt filled areas like this with the freed inmates, and gave them businesses, such as nurseries, to help them get back into civilization. One very successful such nursery sits across the street from us. The workers adore Shirelle, and have rescued her numerous times when she's gotten out, and she of course is crazy about them (likes people in general, but guys who work in soil all day are the best!).

At one point, a complaining neighbor tries to close the nursery down. The owners are shocked when I appear at the City Council hearing on their behalf. They win, and the neighbor grumbles for years.

Moral of the Story: You want someone on your side? Save their dog.

*

The veterinarians insist that I not take Shirelle to a dog park until she is six months old. So her half-year birthday gift is a trip to the largest one in the area. She's thrilled and runs off the second I loosen her leash.

But then she doesn't know what to do. She runs up to bigger dogs: "Hi, I'm here! Play with me!" And they ignore her, walk away, even bark at her to leave them alone. It's every one of us that first day at a new school – scared, eager, hurt.

And then, just as we do at school, she learns the tricks. Whom to approach, how to play, what to do and not. Within a couple of months, she's found her alpha self, loving being chased by dogs around the perimeter till she turns and tumbles with them, joyously biting and chewing and being mauled.

I figure Disneyland could be sued for false advertising; this is inarguably The Happiest Place on Earth.

*

A dream: I'm at my childhood home again, visiting with Shirelle. It's clouding up, one of those big dark clouds, and starting to rain. She's not allowed inside, so we put her in Ygor's old doghouse, and it collapses around her. The wood is too old and waterlogged, and she's too big for it. We all laugh and put her in the garage instead, but suddenly she is too big for it, too. Her head is up in the turrets of the house, and she's pushing through the roof, shingles falling, wood breaking. Still growing.

*

I'm in a hurry. I shove her in the back seat of the car and slam the door. She yelps – I've shut her tail in it!

She stares at me in shock. "I can't believe you did something that hurt me!"

I'm so moved. I've never known a dog before that didn't assume pain from people. She truly thought I was incapable of harm. It's okay that she learned I'm not perfect, but I love that she knows I'm not cruel.

*

She acts on my desires, or so it seems. Sure, she likes my friends, and might feel my fear of a stranger and react to that. But it's more.

We'll be outside, and an attractive woman will walk down the sidewalk. And does Shirelle greet her politely? Or jump on her and try to play? No, she'll leap at the woman, stick her head under her skirt and kick up. Never once has she done that to a woman whom I didn't find sexy. You tell me. Should I feel proud or guilty?

*

I loved photographing her. Made pictures of her into Christmas cards every year of her life. They gained a popularity, with people who hadn't even met me putting her on their wall. Her energy was so big, this just seemed natural.

*

There once was a yard. Full of grass and birds and squirrels and little bugs and some weeds.

Then there was a dog. And the grass began to disappear. And holes to appear.

Sometimes other dogs visited. The grass flew away.

Then the yard was dirt, with trees remaining. Still some birds and squirrels and bugs, but no grass or even weeds.

Then the ground was plowed, and seeded and fertilized.

No luck.

Then new sod was laid.

Lasted weeks.

More holes.

Once there was a yard.

Then there was a puppy.

Game over. No Contest.

*

After hiking a mile or two along a distant beach one day, we see a young woman eagerly scaling a rock, maybe 30 feet high. I turn to Shirelle and comment that we may have found a human equivalent to her. As we approach, I see that she sports a large tattoo on her chest. "Yeah, that'd be you."

We go on, and after a while I sit down and Shirelle runs off. I think about this and that and life and such and five or ten minutes go by… and when I open my eyes… no Shirelle. This isn't like her; she always hangs around. I look up and down the beach, no sign. There couldn't be dognappers here, could there? Then suddenly I see:

Atop that large rock, the woman is sitting up, overseeing her reign, and next to her rises this grand noble beast looking out to the ocean. It's glorious, and beautiful, and strong. The athlete lays her hand on Shirelle's side; they are The Woman Who Runs with the Wolf.

I stand and watch them. Shirelle gazes out to the sea, and then momentarily notices me. She pauses, her head turns quizzically. And suddenly she jumps and runs down to me.

For a few minutes, she'd literally forgotten me. Until the moment of recognition, she had found The Call of the Wild, in the arms of this tattooed climber. When I got back to the rock, the woman told me what a great dog I had. I concurred, and found sticks to heave into the water for her as we headed homeward.

My dog again.

My dog who stayed by me, even in my dreams, at the loneliest time of my life, whom I left behind when I ran away to New Orleans, Houston, Memphis, Miami, but was always there when I got back, who rode with me to Vail and Kansas City, who licked my newborn nephew's mouth, who ripped up the yard and made me dive into the dirt trying to fix it, and who ran alongside greyhounds equaling their speed (at least until they turned).

My dog. And so much more.

In fact, it would now be impossible to ever again see her as my inferior. Her spirit, her generosity, her heart, were above mine. Her brain I still saw as useless, but, at the least, she was worth watching. This silly mutt now was a sort of role model. My Knucklehead, while also the Grand Wolf of the Rock.

Part Two:

Role Model

Chapter Seven:
Love and Romance

Others kept trying to define our relationship. She was my child, my girlfriend, even my wife. I saw her more as a Guardian Angel.

But she had a love, a true love. A boyfriend.

The dog of her life was an Akita-Chow mix she met at the dog park. Kuma (Japanese for bear) was an antisocial rescue, who could only be petted by his patient owner Laura. Outside of her, his life had been endless misunderstanding, until he met Shirelle. It took a few encounters, but they figured each other out. And once they did, no other pooch had a chance to be included. Every meeting was an explosion: Shirelle as alpha female, thrilled to be chased by alpha male Kuma, beating the senses out of each other whenever he caught up.

Occasionally they would have play dates at homes together, with not a second's rest, giving Laura and me the blessing of exhausted dogs at night. When one of us would leave town, and play dates stretched into sleepovers, the equation improved: Three days of Kuma = One week of Shirelle asleep!

On one occasion, I noticed both, in my back yard, covered in mud. This was interesting, since it hadn't rained. In their beating each other to smithereens, they had broken open a water pipe, which now gushed like a fireplug. Didn't even slow them down.

For all my griping about Shirelle's wake of damage over the years, even when she tripped me down a hill and rendered my arm unusable for weeks, I got off easy. One day at the dog park, Kuma accidentally slammed into Laura from behind. She fell onto her tailbone, cracked it, and was in a body cast for months. The doctors told her that if the angle of the fall had been one degree different, she would have had the same injury as Christopher Reeve.

And not that much later, Kuma was peeing red, leading to the discovery of a grapefruit-sized tumor in his kidney. It was removed, but his stomach soon followed, and he had to be put down.

And not long after that, Laura married a wonderful man, who tolerated my speech about Kuma at their wedding, and the multitude of crazy dogs that shared their bed happily ever after.

*

Shirelle had matured and learned manners, so greetings were no longer lethal. But that didn't mean they were peaceful. Like most dogs, she would discover someone visiting or returning, and explode. Screaming joy to the world, her torso leaping, twisting, pulled by her giant-hummingbird heart, with the rest of her just a tail yanked along in bounce.

Who else tells us we're so important? Who says your walking into the room throws them into paroxysms of ecstasy? We know of movie stars or pop singers who can't enter a public place without fans screaming and fainting. But what of the rest of us? Who tells us we're the most exciting and relevant thing in the world?

So why don't we do it for each other? The last time someone you adore walked into the room, how did you act? Did you leap up and let your heart show what it felt? Or were you cool? (Cool. One step from cold. The opposite of life.)

And why are we cool? Because we expect the same from the other. So the one being I was able to treat the way Shirelle treated us all, with explosive thrill at each hello, was, of course, Shirelle.

*

I wonder if dogs have any sense of beauty at all. They have a strong associative sense, and want to be around those with whom they associate good things, via smell, behavior, experience. They preen, licking themselves, rolling in stink, making themselves what they want to be. And they adore – Shirelle could spend hours lying on the floor just gazing at me or other friends. And of course they have preferences when it comes to food.

But is there an *aesthetic* sense? I ask because of her beauty. Certainly a dog's beauty has no evolutionary purpose (some might say beauty makes a dog more likely to survive in a human world, but how does that argument account for bulldogs or Boston terriers?). Outside of my bathing her, brushing her coat, or cutting her nails, and occasional dental cleanings, I did nothing for her looks. Yet no creature has ever been more beautiful.

It wasn't just me. Strangers on the street would say it, people passing by restaurants, "What a beauty!" "May I pet him? He's so beautiful!" Apparently, she never knew what they were saying or feeling. She probably learned that sitting politely got more petting than barking did, but the beauty was unconscious.

One could argue the case of her wide eyes, her long legs, her interesting pattern of orange and white. But that wasn't it. The beauty was something far deeper. I believe that it came from a relaxed confidence. She had no doubts about her attractiveness, only concerns about how others might treat her. So she never hid or did anything "partly." Everything was full. All the Way, or Nothing at All: That's Life. A nice-looking person doing something halfway doesn't draw attention. That same person consumed gets magazine covers.

There were moments when she reached an otherworldly majesty. But even the rest of the time, her beauty never faltered. She slept beautiful, she ran beautiful, she barked at squirrels beautiful. Infused with her spirit, her teeth could make me gasp with their profound primal power tempered by love. Her shed hair was an annoying mess, until you looked closely at it and saw the varying shades, the delicacy and strength. Nothing of her lacked beauty. And the overall was astounding.

One of the most stunning women I've ever known, an emotional whirlwind loaded with talent, had no reason not to be a successful actress and model. Except that whenever the camera took her picture, her heart pulled back. Photos missed her passionate ego, and showed only cold passive fear. I loved the frightened, funny, angry core she hid, as many others loved her great figure and bone structure. But when age devalues the gifts they appreciated, I wonder how many will seek what I had found.

Shirelle hated cameras, and would always look away when I tried to take her picture (the photos in this book tend to be exceptions; luckily I took hundreds). But her heart never hid. A blurred photo of her looking away still revealed her truth, and as Mr. Keats told us, that's beauty, and all ye need to know about it.

*

Abandonment was her deepest fear, so my leaving town always created misery. She could never stand kennels, no matter how nice. To her, a fancy doggy day-care was just my returning her back to the pound. She wouldn't eat or sleep, and would hurt herself trying to climb up chain-link fences to escape. So, instead, I found friends to house-sit, all grateful to me for paying them, but more so for the time with her magic heart. Always that smile, that laugh, filled from within, whenever I'd ask, "So how did it go?" And tolerance and understanding of my need to call twice a day to check.

Meanwhile, Shirelle would adapt by becoming less connected to me, more independent. So that when I returned, she'd hang out in the yard longer, pay more attention to neighbors and vermin, and sleep farther away.

As emotional protection, it worked; only when she'd first see that I was leaving her would she sink into the deep melancholy. Such as when I pulled luggage out.

Which, of course, would turn to thrilled excitement if I put her in the back seat of the car – then it wasn't abandonment, but adventure.

*

Dogs can't hug. People hug dogs, dogs get hugged.

But sometimes, Shirelle hugged me. Stood up on her hind legs, put her forelegs around me, pulled her chest into mine, and pressed her neck and head to me.

Sweet like a child's butterfly kisses, but… no one had ever taught her how to do it.

Dogs can't hug. But the nicest things in the world are Shirelle hugs.

*

Shirelle and I were dog-parking, and she was having a fine time. The belle of the giant ball, she sought out playmates – ideally ones who would chase her around, or just join her for great sniffs – of course checking back on me every once in a while.

This one day, however, love was in the air. A bulldog mix set his eye on her fine figure and decided, "That is the girl for me." While she was drinking some water, he approached behind her and grabbed onto her haunches.

She pulled away, and his feet cheerfully fell to the ground. She went back to some other dogs, and he made another lunge. She pulled away again, turning and giving him a look – did he want to chase her? She ran in a small circle, and he followed. Great! But when she stopped, he climbed onto her backside again. She jerked away with a bark of annoyance, and walked off toward other dogs.

47

With "I'm Gonna Make You Love Me" singing in his heart, he ran up and gave another try. This time she turned and nipped him: "I said, *Stop It!*" He backed off, surprised. She walked away.

Knowing she must just be playing hard to get, he ran up and pulled himself onto her pelvis, with a giant smile on his face.

That was it. Her hair shot up along her spine, her ears flattened, and she spun around, teeth bared. Barking viciously, she chased the terrified mongrel across the park, hell-bent. When he'd fled far enough away, she relaxed, turned to me, and cheerfully trotted back, ears up and flopping, tail in the air, looking for what might be fun to do next.

I have always regretted that no one had a camera on her that day. What a great educational film that would be. How many young teens are confused by mixed signals from family, friends, and media, and go into their first dealings with hormonal suitors with no sense of real self? They reject innocent advances out of fear, or agree to things they aren't remotely ready for because they think they should.

Here was Shirelle's perfect and beautiful lesson: What Every Youngster Needs to Know About Sex and Dating. (I'll state this in the usual boy-girl dynamic, but any apply.) If the boy wants to play on your terms, great. If he wants more, be friendly but pull away. If he keeps trying, he doesn't mean any disrespect; he's doing exactly what he should, so you only have to say no. If it happens again, say it firmly – make sure he gets the point, no matter how desirous or dumb he is. Then, if it happens yet again, beat the @$%#! out of him and scare him into submission. He deserves it, and you'll make life better for another girl somewhere down the line.

*

We knew each other in so many ways, as if all our lives. Had a boyfriend twice her age, but I was no threat – no way I'd step back into that cesspool.

So why, when she bumped into me for the first time in months, did she greet Shirelle coolly with, "Aren't you spoiled!"

I smiled. "Yes, but really, she spoils me."

As she walked away, I thought, that girl's jealous! Wouldn't she be happy to have someone who does for her what I do for Shirelle? Who just asks love and loyalty in return, and not games?

Six months later, our bond yet tighter, she picked me up at the airport after my grandmother's funeral. And took me to a bar, so interested in my experiences, so giving. But stayed in her car as we dropped off my luggage, as she couldn't abide seeing Shirelle and me greet.

*

For some people, what they want is what matters, all the time. For neurotics, being wanted and the lack of it, and the desire for it, and the fear of it, are the only subject. Was that the difference between the Beatles and the Stones? John longing to be wanted (Hold me, love me; Help me if you can) while Mick gloried in raw persistent wanting (Start me up! I can't get no!)?

Shirelle successfully mixed both. She desperately wanted to be wanted, but the second she knew she was, she was fine. And fine meant that she returned to concentrating on her usual agenda: wanting what she wants when she wants it.

Dogs don't sabotage relationships, they don't fear commitment, don't worry about whether they would rather be with someone else. Shirelle never cared about whether I was jealous or not, nor hesitated a second to act on her jealousy in a clear, non-blaming manner. Self-centered, yes. But never codependent or false. Shirelle's great brand of selfishness: The Power of Right Now.

*

An ear
Is to hear
And to balance
Front to rear
To catch the wind
Ride the air
Greet the new
See what's there

Oh! Look at how those
Glider wings
Stick up in shock
Now! See there how they
Pull her face
Down at harsh talk

Such a shape
Such a shape
Every bit is muscles
Frame her head
With a cape
You can view corpuscles

Membrane thin
Soul within
Even when she is asleep
Darting round
Seeking sound
Tiny whispers in will seep:

"I love you
I love you"

Hear it in deep REM
Barely kissed
Makes it twist
Eyes stay shut, not ears, not them.

Ears are most scratchable
Hers are unmatchable.

Chapter Eight:
Creativity and Art

Sure, dogs hear well. But can they appreciate it? What about music?

Ygor never showed any interest in the pop I listened to in his day, but when classical music aired, he would instantly relax in an appreciative high.

Shirelle's music tastes went other directions. Our swinging-tug-of-war evolved to a dance, and if music were playing (the norm in our home), the spins and pulls would be in its energy. That was fine for slow graceful movements, but jumpy numbers set an ecstatic force. To the point that when, say, a Chuck Berry song would come on, she would run and grab the rope, lunging it at me. "Hear that? It's Chuck!"

But the music was changing.

Upon getting Shirelle, I developed a craving for the big band music of the 1930s and '40s. What had once seemed square was now glistening treasure – from the kitsch of postwar Perry Como to complexities by Duke Ellington and Stan Kenton that I couldn't quite "hear" yet, but would learn to over time. From the pure joy of Shaw, Goodman, James, Miller, and new names like Kyser and Thornhill, and the warmest voices ever like Helen Forrest and Dick Haymes, to deepening appreciation for the throats I already knew – Holiday, Sinatra, Cole, Fitzgerald, Crosby, Ink Spots, Millses, the Louises Armstrong and Jordan… it just went on and on.

It affected her, too. I figured that was just because when certain songs played, they'd become ours, as I'd pick up her paws, lay her forearms over my shoulders, and we'd dance. "Who Wouldn't Love You?" Who indeed?

Years later, I developed a yen to play the trumpet. I went to a local music store, bought a beaten old horn, and signed up for lessons.

I already knew that I didn't know how to get my lips to blow right. I didn't realize, though, how hard it would be to learn. Morning and night, day after day, I squawked out the most dreadful sounds imaginable.

I'd wondered if Shirelle would tolerate my practicing, or if her sensitive ears would send her outside every time I picked up the instrument. But she didn't just tolerate it; she *loved* it. From the first time I began squawking, she would walk in, lie on the floor in front of me, and gaze at me with the eyes of a teen idolator throughout. So that my practicing became not just for me, but a reward to her.

So the question arose: Was it just me who loved that music? Or was the whole house filled with an appreciative fandom? Did that dog just plain like the sound of brass? And if so, had my tastes changed on their own, or did she somehow…?

Similarly, as she matured enough to develop eye-mouth coordination and become an excellent catcher and fetcher, I, on a whim, signed up for tennis lessons, where I got fairly good quickly – suddenly losing twenty years of neurotic self-sabotage.

Just what was this connection with this dog all about?!

*

I was barely getting by, with film and television jobs that meant nothing to me, but now daring to try out my new directing skills in small plays, and beginning to grasp what I'd sought in those acting classes – largely due to a tutor I had on the side. A tutor who had absolutely mastered the arts of being in the moment, living truthfully, full commitment, real listening – all these concepts Sanford Meisner brought so brilliantly to actors' training. Though a tutor who didn't know the meaning of concepts like creativity and imagination. But she did know something at least equally valuable.

Even before I met her, the word Knucklehead fit her so well, but why? She wasn't stupid. But she was a Knucklehead. Eventually I came up with a definition:

> *A Knucklehead is someone who might be perfectly smart, but their sweet explosive emotions take over, above and beyond their intelligence.*

A bizarre form of genius, actually.

It certainly is strange to say that the wisest philosopher I ever met was too stupid to know that you can't walk in front of a moving car. But I already knew not to walk in front of cars, so I didn't need to learn that from her. It's all the other things that she was teaching, as I began to define her strength in four simple words:

All
Heart
No
Brain.

*

I was sitting on the floor doing paperwork, when suddenly there was a huge commotion outside. "Hey look!" "Is she going to…?" "WOW! Did you see that?!" "Hey, come here!" "No, don't…" "CAN YOU BELIEVE THAT???"

The dope had been in my back yard, heard my neighbors Jesse and Susan outside, jumped up onto the five-foot fence, and pulled herself over. They were scared she was going to run away, but she ran straight to them, then turned back, leaped, and cleared herself right back into her yard.

She did *what?*

She had attained her adult body. Sixty-five pounds, thin but muscular, with unnaturally tall legs that were far too strong for comfort.

They showed me where she'd come over, and I went to the hardware store and got some fencing to build it up higher.

Mixed emotions: "Stupid dog, I wanted to do other stuff today; this'll take all my free time." Versus, "You got out of the yard and didn't run away? Just wanted to show off to them that you could do it? You angel."

The two reactions do have a similar factor, though: "You knucklehead!"

Weeks later, I was watering flowers in the front yard, when Shirelle walked up to me cheerfully. Hmm, I thought, I've got to fix that back gate. But when I took her back, it wasn't open. Uh oh.

I left her in the back, called her, and sure enough, over a different part of the fence she came, full of childlike pride. I realized I'd need to build yet more fencing. I put her back inside the yard and suddenly she started over again. I said no, she kept coming, and, "%@#&! *NO!*" I pushed her back. She landed fine, but my guts sank: Her face.

The dejection in her eyes. The hurt. She had been so proud of her discovery and achievement, so excited and open, and I was so cold and rejecting.

She was teaching me again. How many times do we all feel that devastation? How much does it stay with us? Is there any cure?

Well, treats help.

*

Shirelle and I took a visiting friend to Malibu and strolled along the beach. Illegally, we kept walking when some signs told us the next stretch was closed to

56

the public. As we ambled, a pair of men appeared on the horizon, coming toward us. So far away it would be a half hour before we passed, so I figured we were safe from being evicted as we got closer.

"Check this out. See, the tall one, he's just dressed normal. But the shorter one, he's in the uniform. Scruffy beard, sunglasses, baseball cap, hunched over. Everywhere you go it's another bozo trying to prove he's Steven Spielberg by dressing like him."

It would be another ten minutes before they were close enough for me to gulp, "Um, never mind." It *was* Spielberg. And that tall guy, that was Tom Hanks. They passed us by, not returning our looks, Spielberg listening while Hanks pontificated on how important a statement this would be, something we needed to be reminded of. A few years on, I'd be pretty sure we had witnessed the genesis of *Saving Private Ryan*.

And later, when we had turned around to head back to the car and they'd headed back as well, and we passed them again, Hanks kept talking, but Spielberg turned and smiled at Shirelle, soaking up her joy.

Actors act. Directors see, and take note of the most valuable images.

*

Theatre Palisades, a beautiful playhouse near my home, advertised for a director. I didn't get the job, but they asked me to put up a one-act play, to show my stuff, and it went over well.

They then asked if I would join them in a local July 4th parade. I'd never cared for parades much, but reluctantly agreed, in hopes of earning a later gig. But then, the eyes across the room: "You're not abandoning me again, are you?" Hey, I could take…

Self-conscious, I strode alongside the float, while she reveled on an extended leash running side to side to sniff people, bark at other dogs, drink watchers' water. And, when my attention wasn't on her, to dive onto the mounds left by earlier marching horses, and roll as strongly and quickly as she could, perfuming herself and earning great cheers from the crowd, who were otherwise getting pretty bored by the 200th entry.

So we walked that parade every July of her life.

*

Have you ever watched a dog's nose? On a relaxed morning, just sitting watching the world go by, enjoying the fresh cool air, she would lie in the doorway (a favorite spot, blocking the door open, to make sure she had access both to squirrels and to anything I might decide to eat). Lying down, yes, but with her chest upright and her eyes, ears, and nose grasping far more information than I was getting from any book, television, or newspaper. Eyes looking for movement, anything strange going on in trees or bushes. Ears tilting and grasping every sound wave that comes through the yard, with the most active part of her brain judging each noise and whether it merited jumping up and barking and running to the fence (and possibly scaring a squirrel from coming down into reach).

"Pay Attention." The number one habit of highly effective animals.

But that nose! Look at her. Look at it. Not the full snout, which includes the upper part of the mouth. Just the little black cold one. See it in action. Moving all 360 degrees, twisting, turning, knowing so many things we never will.

People often say that dog's noses are the equivalent to our eyes. That dogs investigate by smelling as we read or scan. But there's a difference, of intimacy. When we see, we're seeing the light reflecting off of objects, not the objects themselves. Eyes are lenses, ways of picking up information, translated to electrical signals our brain can use. But noses actually absorb the true material. When Shirelle sniffs a rose, or a steak, or a pile of dog poo, she is literally taking in an infinitesimal amount of that substance. It goes into her system. (This is why you can get intoxicated, or even killed, with a smell, whereas sights can only have such an effect through their meaning.)

Humans could do better. We'll notice big odor changes – the neighbors are barbecuing, the jasmine's blooming, a skunk must have been run over up the hill – but do we really pay attention to how the world smells after a rain? Do we appreciate the rich odor of a newly fertilized garden? Do we note each tree? Or the beautiful scents of those people who walk by us? Or, of course, dogs?

In our mindset where scents are mostly considered undesirable, with expensive chemicals used to cover or sterilize them, aren't we really just separating ourselves from the earth, from life? While Shirelle lies on her doormat, concentrated, seeking it.

*

The stinky parade – and months of work – paid off, as that theater hired me to direct John Guare's masterful *Six Degrees of Separation*. The experience was magical. Even during the rehearsals, it was clear that lasting relationships were forming. Dawn, our lead actress, and I developed a closeness not unlike long-lost siblings. And, so different from the drama of the year before, boundaries were clear and unquestioned, as her husband and daughter adopted me into their family.

Oh, and she and Shirelle were nuts about each other too.

Our assistant director had the usual sweet brash honesty of 19-year-olds, so much to say and nothing to block it. At a rehearsal at my house, I asked her to come meet Shirelle. I opened the door, and the Knucklehead jumped up, madly licking her face. She burst out into peals of laughter. "This is perfect! You know how they say people and their dogs look alike?"

"Yeah?"

"Well look at her! She's tall and thin and has a really big nose!"

She stopped laughing, exclaimed, "Oh!" and stared at me in shock. "I shouldn't have said that, should I?"

The production opened fairly well, with the cast exhausted, but by the second weekend, they were *on*. Saturday night, everything in the show clicked, creating a palpable energy that literally changed my life: *I can do this*. I no longer needed to take a back seat to anyone in this craft.

Suddenly, as the curtain shut midway through the play, a huge crash pealed out. Had the set fallen? Were any actors killed? I shot around the building. Thank God, no. It had been a light pole, pulled over by a curtain. The light would be missed that night, but it was reparable, and no one was hurt.

At seven the next morning, Shirelle heard a dog walking by and ran into the living room so hard that she smashed into the window and broke it.

After a year and a half of stagnation, my life was beginning to explode.

*

I'd always cared about what was The Best. In terms of movies, music, etc. But now, that fell apart. As my creative voice newly flourished, I found such cerebral concepts annoying.

Yet, around this time, I still came up with my fullest nickname for her. In pure judgment:

Best Thing Ever
Never Clever
Never Never Ever Clever
Could be smart
But not make art
But lives life deep as art —
That's smart.

But never
Ever
Ever
In the furthest reaches of the imagination
Never
Ever
Clever.

No wit
No lies
No alibis
Never Ever Clever
Best Thing Ever.

Cleverness is an addiction when you do it without choosing to – when I have to make a joke about something, not because it's funny, but because it covers my anxiety.

Cleverness isn't a bad thing, but one of the reasons for the clarity of Shirelle's integrity was her lack of cleverness.

*

Even before *Six Degrees*, everyone was telling me the same thing: I had to make a feature film. Put all the eggs into one basket and get my name out there. Maybe it was from the terror of this next step, but after years of writing for others, my imagination froze – I couldn't come up with any story ideas, much less any good ones.

So I did the only thing I could think of, and put an ad in a number of trade journals, looking for low-budget scripts. Hundreds came in. Some good, some not.

Some set in foreign countries, or sci-fi, clearly not grasping what I meant by low-budget.

Two grabbed my attention most. One was a cute comedy about a guy hired to double a look-alike movie star (a great idea, proven later when it showed up in Steve Martin's *Bowfinger*). The other was a play, with just two characters, all taking place in one room over one afternoon. The tiniest of crises: a beaten-down man discovers that his mother is losing her mind and tries to do something about it. I was fascinated and consumed by the play – its pain, its humor, and its devastating truths.

It would need rewriting, lots. Plays seldom worked as movies, and single-location ones with small casts even less so. But some did – *Rope, Sleuth* – and if I devoted myself to it, it could glow. Our population was aging, the baby boomers were turning 50, and their parents were living longer than anyone in history. Mine could be the movie to open a needed conversation, to break down walls.

And so again I fell in love. But this time, I was in love with beautiful dialogue, with my vision, with all it could be. But love can cost – money, heartbreak, even health. And no love ever cost me as much as this one, on all counts.

Though a true love it was.

Chapter Nine:
Self-Worth

No one can make you irrelevant. If I hadn't paid attention to Bill Gates, that wouldn't have changed a thing in terms of his relevance. If I didn't pay attention to Shirelle, she might have starved, but she wouldn't have been any less relevant, to herself. And she sure found me relevant.

Yet I still felt so irrelevant. Though I planned very strongly that this movie would change all that.

For about a year, I prepared it. I worked with the playwright to "open up" the plot, to bring in characters who had only been references before, and to expand the action from one room to an old house with secrets hidden throughout.

We got the funding, got a crew, and we got a cast. A few friends, a few unknowns, and, for our leads, three great coups – Timothy Bottoms, Kim Greist, and the Oscar-winner the play had been written for, Kim Hunter.

And a couple of instances of nepotism. My niece, and, yes, the Poop-head.

*

A Dream: I'm at this building at the seaside. My room is far upstairs, hard to reach through a very small staircase.

I want to get to a more social area in the back, but I have to go through a tiny window, by pulling the screen out. It leads me into an apartment. Linda Ronstadt is living there, from her "What's New" period. I'm very excited, and try to talk to her, but she's annoyed. Muttering, "You don't care about me. You're just another guy who got hot for the cover of *Hasten Down the Wind*." I follow her and some other people down to the ocean, still trying to talk with her, but no one there wants anything to do with me.

I walk back to the building and see Shirelle waiting underneath it, and we happily go in together.

Relevance waits where you find it.

*

I was mailed an ad for veterinary insurance. The price seemed fair, and I figured it was a great idea. I paid to insure my car, my health, my home – was any of them as likely to run into disaster as the Knucklehead? Of course, the danger is that you might pay the premiums every year while the dog is perfectly healthy, but then just before she gets old, she's pancaked by an uptight neighbor speeding his SUV while dialing his cell phone to pretend he's not late to work. But I figured it was a gamble worth taking.

Paid off too, right away. The day her policy went into effect, she lunged against the fence to greet my neighbors and broke her toe.

I ran her to the local emergency animal hospital, and they x-rayed her and proceeded to fix her up, while I sat in the lobby watching their television. It was showing *The Piano*. I'd liked that movie very much. However, I'd forgotten about how Sam Neill exacted his punishment on Holly Hunter, and when that scene came, my heart ossified: What are they *doing* to my baby back there?

She got a cast on her front left paw, which would slide a bit on the floor when she stepped onto it. Over the next weeks, she'd walk across floors, click click thump click, click click thump click, and never complain, just do what she had to, as dogs always do. It's her adaptability. Expressed her distress, and then opted for the best possible alternative.

Such a teacher.

*

All was going as well as possible with preparing the movie – only a few crises per day – when I went to my doctor for a checkup. I mentioned a spot below my navel that was hurting a little, probably a bruise from a large belt-buckle. He felt it and said the two words one least wants to hear from their physician, "Uh" and "Oh."

I'd never heard of an umbilical hernia before. Apparently due to my being "pulled off" too roughly by the nurse who severed me after my first spank, my intestines were sticking through a tiny rupture in my abdominal wall. It didn't bother me much, and I'd have been happy to wait to have it operated on after the movie was shot. But he insisted waiting could result in infection or even death, so within a couple of days, I was in major surgery.

What had been a tiny annoyance was now huge – my belly swelled up with trauma and fluid to where I looked eight months pregnant, and I was loaded with post-op drugs, including Vicodin, bearing warnings that it could cause drowsiness or nausea.

It did neither. It served as a euphoric so I could cheerfully feel that someone was in pain, but it really wasn't me. However, it also arrested my short-term memory. To where I couldn't remember conversations five minutes after they took place.

The operation affected Shirelle profoundly. The lap-running endless energy burner now slept twenty-two hours a day against me – when possible, against the wound. For the other two hours, sure, a turbine on amphetamines, but otherwise just a healer. As Dawn brought me meals, and the production staff managed to keep the movie on track, Shirelle gave of her energy, her life. Precious and unthinking, her deepest gift and all she could give.

Most of the time I'm sure it helped, too. Except the point in the wee wee hours each night, when I was sleeping well and the Vicodin had worn off, with her warm against my belly, when her tight legs would need a good stretch, and she'd push her whole spine right into my stitches and engorged tissues, ripping deep sleep with a bloodcurdling scream out of me that shocked us both equally.

*

Dogs are great in families. But this one-on-one relationship was something different. It's not that Wolfgang or Ygor hadn't been capable of this connection, but the dynamic wasn't right for it. Shirelle and I had developed a different bond, a closeness impossible in a larger pack. She was still a knucklehead, and I was still a goof, but we – the pair of us – *that* was becoming something kind of amazing.

*

Another dream: I am in a large mall, on the top of many floors, and see Bob Dylan heading down the escalator. I go to follow him, always having wanted to meet him, but on the way down I see, coming up the other side, a romance from the past, a woman I'd loved, but learned to distrust.

I turn and start running up the escalator, to get away from her. As hard as I can, feeling her gaining, till I run so hard I run the escalator right out of the building, into space, where it flaps around like a loose fan belt, with me running at the end of it.

I woke knowing exactly what it meant. Dylan had recently put out his phenomenal *Time Out of Mind*, and his songs of walking dirt roads bound in cold irons symbolized pure truth and integrity to me. And that woman was lies – beautiful, sexy, intoxicating, titillating, lies. And I was running from them for dear life.

I was making a movie, but it was not going to be lies. I wanted the dirt road, and I ran from anything that would falsify it.

Emulating Shirelle. So beautiful, but all true. No glamour, no lies. And she loved dirt roads. She'd track them in anywhere.

*

Although Hunter had played the lead in the original play a few years before, she attacked her role as new. Specifically, she worked to understand the manifestations of dementia – what does it feel like, how does one react to it – and to break down the script with decisions of what's happening in her at every moment. She was the oldest of us, but had no idea what aging is like, such a vibrant soul. But she had a perfect coach: Thanks to the Vicodin, I had just lived senility firsthand.

She and I rehearsed for one week together, without any other actors, digging through every word wherever we could – in a theater's rehearsal space, in restaurants, and in my home, where she was greeted with the usual cyclone by my roommate. I explained to her that this was to be her costar for one day, and she glared at me for the first time with scorn and shock, over her reading glasses, and in her precise diction pursed out, "You. Must. Be. In. *Sane!*"

I wasn't. The role was perfect for Shirelle – bad dog misbehaving and getting yelled at – and she did beautifully. But my high point of her day on set was when I introduced her to lovely Miss Greist, who flushed on seeing her: "Would it be all right if I kissed her on the nose?"

I could have proposed that instant – one other person in the world who had exactly my reaction to that face!

*

After Shirelle's successful shoot, we still had two and a half weeks of filming to go. Waking at four a.m. every day (invariably with a start, convinced I'd overslept), and watching footage late into the night, I was the most absent I would ever be from her. As always, she adjusted to my behavior, and became more independent – happy to see me when I came home, but then pursuing her other interests right away.

Her main fascination was rats. A number of them were living in my neighbor's yard, but enjoyed my garage as a vacation condo. Each evening, they would walk the phone and power line routes between the two, which included a journey through our orange tree. She would jump as high as she could, trying to catch them (she'd do this for birds during the day, too, but it got much more frantic when the nocturnal invaders came out). As dusk turned into darkness, she couldn't tell what was a rodent and what was just a breeze rustling the leaves. But she knew what she wanted it to be. So the jumping was constant, for hours. And when I'd turn in, for whatever sleep I could steal, she would join me happily snoring away. I was failing at being there for her, but she was succeeding at her primary job – living.

After the shooting ended, I was still on the phone or in the editing room continually. Until one Saturday, when I could get to all the paperwork I'd ignored for a month. And Shirelle climbed onto… the couch.

Not by accident, and not sneakily. She stared at me the whole time, as she deliberately pulled herself up paw by paw and lounged on the taboo white throne, daring me. "So, will you notice me *now?*"

Message received. I yelled at her to get off, she did, and I dropped all I was doing, gave her a huge rubdown, and took her outside to play fetch, as the hernia, the movie, and the bills all stepped aside for a far higher calling.

A good thing, too. As the months of intensity required to make a good product evolved into years of endless slogging to get it seen and marketed, it was time to get back into my real world.

*

The drive from L.A. to the Rocky Mountains is nerve-racking in parts, boring in others, and interminable in one. A stretch of more than a hundred miles in eastern Utah with few turns and virtually no humanity. It only makes sense to pull over after that, when you hit the first towns of Colorado, leading to Grand Junction.

On this January day, I had relied on the car's cruise control and figured that if I didn't stop just yet, we might make it in time to see my niece and nephew before they went to bed. As the road reduced to two lanes on either side, with drop-offs on the shoulders, I sensed that the speed limit should be going down, but since it didn't, I stayed just over the posted 75. I passed a restaurant twenty-six miles in, and turned to see if it would be open when we returned early in a few mornings. When I turned back, I saw that I was starting to lead the car off the left side of the highway. I pulled the steering wheel to the right, and the car straightened out.

Then suddenly the whole world flipped.

All I remember is flashes. Spinning. Across the lanes, me screaming…

And the next image is that we've crashed into the retaining guardrail, hard. Really hard. All had smashed. Broken glass everywhere, both air bags had popped, and inside the car all was chaos. And we're crosswise, across I-70, and a truck is coming. And we're about to die.

But the truck slows down, and passes *in front* of us (we'd hit the guard rail so hard we'd bounced back) and stops.

I looked at Shirelle, who was staring back at me, and got out (I'm ashamed to say I didn't think to get her out at once too, in case of fire). There was smoke everywhere. The fender was twenty feet away. The radiator was smashed in. The windows weren't cracked, but there was broken glass along the bottoms of them, like snow.

And then, as I looked at the car, a voice in my head said, "This is okay." It was yet another explosion, moving on from the past, a step forward. Though at that moment, with the horrible scene in front of me, it was a really strange sentence to hear.

If the spinout had been ten yards farther down, there wouldn't have been a guardrail, and we would have careered over a hillside and into some storage sheds; probably I would have been killed and Shirelle would have lived. If we'd hit the guardrail, but Shirelle hadn't been fastened to my car's seatbelt with a harness I'd found at an overpriced pet store, she would be dead. Either immediately, from being thrown through the windshield, or injured so badly I'd have had to put her to sleep. And if another vehicle had been closer, we both would have been killed. Not to mention whomever we took out.

For the next few days, I'd awaken with starts reliving the accident, struggling to figure out what had happened. Eventually I arrived at this: I had the cruise control on. When I saw myself veering off the left of the road, I pulled to the right. My foot didn't instinctively go to the brake, which would have automatically shut the control off. Instead, the sudden jerk to the right forced the car to slow down, so the cruise control *accelerated*. Meanwhile, the car was off balance – so it accelerated *into* the imbalance, causing the spin out of control and across the highway.

Cruise control is a great metaphor for "leaning" in life. My instinct had told me, less than a minute before the accident, that I was going too fast. But because the speed limit sign read 75, I trusted that posting, instead of my feeling, and this happened. I had lived way too much of my life in cruise control, and it was time to change.

The truck had pulled over. I walked up to its door, where a woman was calling the police. She asked if I was okay. I said yes. Other people stopped, also asking. I got Shirelle out and tied her to the truck.

A police officer showed, put up flares, and let me put Shirelle in the back of his car. Finally, I was coming "down to earth" enough to comfort her in her nervous panting (while also looking at that big mug in the back of a squad car and thinking, "About time!").

The woman in the truck told me she was on her way to Denver with her husband, and offered to wait till I was able to go, and then drive us to my brother's exit. They even gave Shirelle their leftovers from dinner.

The tow truck driver told me the car was totaled. The officer handed me his card, revealing his name – Steven King – grinning, "I'm just another part of your nightmare!"

I emptied all my goods from the car, put Shirelle into the truck, and we set off, with me holding her tight.

We rode together for three hours. The driver talked about her history, with a lot of really bad accidents, and how there'd always been someone to help her, so she was just doing payback. As she dropped us off, she returned my thanks with, "Pass it on."

I knew how to obey. My payback would be to buy all the seatbelt harnesses I could, and give them to every friend who had a dog. And to preach the harness gospel forever, in gratitude.

A few days later, in a rented car, we headed back to L.A. We left very early, and Shirelle slept for three hours, until we got near the place of the accident.

Suddenly she bolted up, panting and pulling on the harness, struggling to get out of the car. I tried my best to calm her, but couldn't get past my shock: Was it smell, or some canine GPS? Whatever it was, she knew that location *in her sleep*.

*

Six months later, I dared to head back, to a family camping trip. Stopping at a gorgeous view along the way. Rocky cliffs. She's so excited by the smells, is all focused down, sniffing, led by her nose, hurriedly, this way and that, sniff, sniff, sniff, sniff, and she gets to the edge, sniff, sniff, her head goes past it, sniff, and I almost grab her, but suddenly she sees how far down it is − her focus adjusts from four inches to hundreds of feet − and her ears shoot up, her chest sticks out, her head swings around, and she gawks at me in shock.

Astoundingly, Shirelle again recognized Grand Junction and got anxious. As I drove through, I noticed a cool-looking car. And then I looked back at the road, and realized I was veering off again. But I was going 65 miles an hour, so we were fine. I had passed a sign that said 75, but I *felt like* going 65.

My gut had said the same thing in January. But now, having followed my instinct like Shirelle, I was able to turn the car back to the right, and drive smoothly the long and winding road to their door.

We are all told, many times in life, that our inner voice is not good, or right. But not once has that voice in me been wrong. Many say it's never been wrong in anybody. Shirelle had been showing me how to listen for four years, and at last I was beginning to pick up on the lessons. To treat that inner voice as relevant.

Some camping trips stink − everyone's in lousy moods, tires blow, mosquitoes reenact The Ride of the Valkyries, people drink to get along and then suffer miserable hangovers. Some trips are just fine, and afterwards all involved congratulate themselves on "how nice it was." And some just sing.

I've never seen a more beautiful camping spot, and while my brother apologizes endlessly for the rain, cool foggy mist with occasional drizzle in August is our idea of heaven. I love the sights, and, lordamighty, does Shirelle love the smells. So many new things to chase, and who cares if they fly or climb, it's the chase that matters.

One morning Shirelle wants us to throw sticks to fetch. After a while, we tire of this, but she's just getting warmed up. I pick up a branch, maybe seven feet long, twenty pounds, and throw it down a hillside, nearly steep enough to call a cliff, figuring she'll chase it, struggle, and give up and find something else to do.

But a minute later, from out of deep woods, up gallops the Knucklehead, the branch in her mouth, puffing and puffing, leaping upwards with every step. Everyone is astonished, none more than I, she in an ecstasy transcending corporeal form. I take the branch from her, heave it again, and down she goes, overjoyed. Time and time again, pounding her legs, chest shoving with each reach, lungs squeezing her up that incline with such thin air, such joy, such joy.

Later, we pack up while she romps off for a hunt. When she comes back, I could weep. She has rolled in something, something awful, pungently disgusting. I know I can't get it all off of her.

I soap and scrub her all I can, but the residue stays there. Everyone is going to hate her on the long drive down.

And then, the sun sticks out, just a bit, through the clouds. And the world just ignites. I grab my camera, and snap all I can.

She is breathtaking. Partly because her body looks so strong and dramatic – from all my scrubbing. But it's also what's in her. She feels strong, noble. She ran that branch up that mountain so many times, and now she smells of something she finds fantastic. Hundreds gasped at the image, while only a few knew the truth behind it.

And even we didn't know the full truth. The great terror: Each camper had paid a little visit to the woods that morning. Could it be we had smelled the enemy, and it was one of us?

*

On the drive back to L.A., she was relaxed the whole way. She whined a bit as I exited at mile 26 for a bite, but that may have been just the thrill at seeing we'd be getting out for a walk and a sniff.

Chapter Ten:
Life to the Fullest

The Stare.

The ears perfectly perpendicular, straight out, airplane wings.

The body at attention. Tensed, or at ease, but ready.

The eyes fully connect to mine. No deficit, she is focused. Nothing I say or do escapes her. She even notes my scent.

Nothing between us but wills. She wants, and I'm letting her or not.

We are in sync.

We may not know why the other says or wants, but we know their wish. And feel the intensity.

*

She went into everything with ardor, even sleep. When people, and most animals I've seen, sack out, it's a relaxation, often in ridiculous form, an expression of exhaustion. But she slept with a ferocity, eyes clamped shut, body straight out or curled up in a cozy oval, or even lying prone with her head relaxed on her forepaws – always with an attention, an intention. She went into sleep as she entered a forest or field, embracing what was to come. Sleep was a treat, a reward, a meal, an adventure.

*

The Hiding Place found universal acclaim, though it was still struggling to find a distributor willing to handle such dramatic material. But I was sure it was too good not to sell, and meanwhile was happily busy directing – from lots of stage projects, to a music video of some friends' band, to some public service ads, one starring The Knucklehead.

Life was on the upswing, though I still felt no deep direction. My new motto was "Everything's negotiable but Shirelle."

*

And as my creative output increased and my confidence grew, something came back into my life that had seemed almost extinct: Women.

I was dating, a lot. And the women around me who had seemed unreachable suddenly were there. Through tennis, old friendships, friends of friends, the impossible became suddenly possible.

The soulmate who drove me nuts with her draw to men she feared, till one day, sitting in a church I was using as a film location, I asked for help and a voice came to me saying, "You're not enough;" the hourglass charmer who took me to grand Hollywood parties and seemed so of-another-time I expected her to introduce me to Clara Bow and Rudy Vallee; the hilarious sexy neurotic with the daughter who fell madly in love with Shirelle and would walk up to strangers, pointing at me and saying "That man is not my father," and just before they called a cop, would add, "He's my mom's friend and he has the bestest dog in the world!"

Meanwhile, given how many women complained about my attachment to Shirelle, it's amazing how many would, when breaking up with me, ask to come by when I wasn't there, so they could play and hang out with her.

At least I had good taste in women with good taste.

But none lasted. All fell apart, for one reason or another. And the harder I loved, the harder I'd fall, one and all.

But just because I was miserable didn't mean Shirelle had to be. So I'd take her to the dog park, and she'd run around, while I'd sit, deep in it.

A standard poodle walks by. I glance up to see the owner. It's Jack Lemmon. I give him a smile of quiet recognition. He turns away in fear.

At least Shirelle's happy, anyway.

*

She often wandered behind a big palm tree in a back corner of my yard, checking out smells. But occasionally she spent an inordinate amount of time there.

Eventually, I met a neighbor from the next street. Evelyn had spent the last few years caring for her ailing husband, watching his faculties deteriorate. He had lost some memory, but didn't seem delusional at all, until he began telling her about his visions. "I was sitting here today, looking out the window, and saw a yellow dog playing in the garden." She scolded him lightly, pointing out that he could see perfectly well that there was no dog in their yard, and it was all fenced in. But still on other days he would tell her "the yellow dog came again." Perhaps it was a harbinger, she pondered. And when he did pass on, she thought about what that yellow dog might have signified.

Until a few weeks later when she was working in her garden, and the Knucklehead bounded in, through an opening she'd worked in the fence, and jumped on her. Probably would have been sure it was her husband coming back for a kiss, if the goofball hadn't had ID tags.

*

Shirelle never picked a fight. She'd sometimes get jealous if I petted another dog too much, and run over and dominate it with a lesson about who's the alpha. And there was the time she was locked outside and saw my parents' lab eating out of her bowl, and eight hours later remembered it at their next meeting and opened up some #@$% on her. And there was always the great show of fury when she and another dog were on leashes and had to impress each other. But she never wanted to fight.

In the dog park, when a brawl would break out, most dogs would run toward it, to get included, or at least investigate, while Shirelle would cheerfully walk the opposite direction, looking for anything else to interest her. Yet after Annie's attack in her early days, she won every altercation but one in her life. And she'd win, not by fighting, but by ending the fight.

It was so simple. A dog would attack her, and she would use her length, height, and speed to get above it, and force it to the ground. Instantly her long mouth was open, clamped onto the other dog's throat. The dog would stop moving at once, feeling its hopes for the future suddenly fragile. And when it had calmed enough for her, she'd let go and back away. Sometimes the other dog chose to ignore her, or play in a way she liked. And if so, she was perfectly agreeable. But if not, if the dog went in for another attack, exactly the same action would recur. Sometimes they'd learn. Sometimes they wouldn't, and embarrassed owners would have to just take their losers away from her.

But I wonder if any martial art teaches a higher level of skill, honor, or warrior morality than this. Or one that could possibly make a parent prouder.

*

When people think, at least after reaching a certain age, we do so in words. Even if we have primarily visual or kinesthetic minds, our brains still use a language when we perceive the world ("Wow, she's hot!") or react to it ("Ouch!" or "That idiot!").

But isn't there a deeper language in us? Shirelle viewed the world through a lens I don't. Not just in terms of having less color in her eyesight, but in what she focused on, what she picked up from things, and especially what they meant to her. And it's more than a lens. Lenses only affect what you see; Language (in this sense) determines the meaning of all you experience, and thereby how you respond to it.

I see people who only experience the world in terms of what things mean to them or about them – they hear and speak a Language of Narcissism. Others who live everything through and about their religion – they have a Language of Faith (While there are millions more who speak the words of faith, but are only pretending to truly experience that language).

I guess Shirelle's language, at this time in her life, was all about what she wanted at that second. But that might mature.

What, I wondered, was mine?

*

I found some reel-to-reel tapes of my family, from my childhood and before. On one, my father is using my two-year-old fingers to play "Chopsticks." As the song ends, I shriek with glee. Shocked at what I'd done, thrilled at the giant hands manipulating mine into perfect odd harmony.

That kid was open, totally vulnerable. Hearing that recording decades later, I felt a jolt of fear. Fear at such openness.

It's about *play*. When I'd write, or especially when I'd direct or act, there would be play in it. But what I created would always be just a bit safe, not that vulnerable. I couldn't trust enough to let myself go that far.

Ygor had always had a neurotic fear of rejection, so he'd get so excited whenever anyone walked up to him that he'd pee on them. Now that's vulnerable. But Ygor never learned how to play. No one ever taught him.

Shirelle assumed everyone would like her. She'd been wrong and gotten hurt at times, but when she was right, she got to play a lot. I'd taught her games, and we'd invented games together.

So if I knew enough to teach play, then what did she have that I lacked?

It was the *initiating*. I could play, but only on others' terms. I didn't allow myself to initiate play in the "Love To A Fault" way that Shirelle did, whether at the right or wrong moment. And, worse, I couldn't judge the other's reaction as healthily as she.

I had always told myself that my failed attempts at social interaction were because something was wrong with me. Shirelle never felt that. She would say, "I'll get another ball; maybe that'll work." Or, "It's too bad that they don't want to play. I'll have to wait for someone else to come along now."

I'd taught her games, but she was teaching me how to play.

Or at least she was trying to. If I could just grasp what she knew.

*

ACT TWO

SCENE FOUR. LIVING ROOM.

Afternoon. A beautiful day.

The man walks in from stage left carrying a cordless phone.

MAN: Oh it's a gorgeous day here. How've you been? Good.

He casually walks to the open front door and leans on the jamb, soaking up the beautiful weather.

MAN: Yeah, I'm just … What? Oh! She's seen a squirrel! Wait, I think she's gonna catch… OH MY #&@%^$! SHE'S

80

```
CLIMBING THE TREE!  I swear, she's… No, she didn't make it
all the way up, but she climbed that #$@%! tree!  She must
have gotten eight feet up there!

Enter SHIRELLE, proudly strutting into the house looking
for excitement.

MAN:  Knucklehead!  What are you?!
```

*

And then, after so many years, it happened. As if overnight.

The Hiding Place got written up in *Playboy*, of all places, and was now being looked at by very interested distributors, while Hunter and Bottoms were naming it publicly as their best work. I was earning a living making low-budget music videos for the Japanese and Vietnamese markets. I directed a production of *Company*, daring not just a musical but one very close to my heart, which became my greatest theatrical success. While more precious to me was a little two-person romantic comedy I wrote and directed, about how we seem to always fall in love with the same people.

More precious because, at last, I was at the fully creative place I had sought. Still safe, perhaps, but nothing felt held back. My creativity flowed 100 percent, clear, with self-doubt never soiling the result.

And on one day, *Company* and *Purgative* were both performed, on different sides of L.A., at the same time. Neither one paid me any money, or got sizable press. But the part of me that had taken decades to find, to train, to polish, had achieved a goal: I had a voice at last. Now all I needed was to…

…And then, just as quickly, it turned, and crashed into rubble.

Within a few months, the 1990s boom economy collapsed into recession, taking all the companies that had been hiring me, or even thinking about it, out of business; the movie got rejected by every distributor; the music video of my friends' band helped them get a great recording contract, which included re-recording that song, meaning my video became an instant antique, and the producers hired a more established director to promote them; the successful runs of *Company* and *Purgative* were over, bringing no boosts to my career – I'd never even managed to sign an agent, and was getting no younger – making me a nobody in this business; some old friends who'd found success stopped returning my phone calls, apparently now considering me beneath them; and a show I'd spent more than a year writing, for a group that had promised to put it up, was rejected.

Eventually, many of the group members confessed that it had never had a chance. They were just carrying too much negativity, after their biggest and most difficult production ever. Within months, their company fell apart.

But by the time I learned that, it was too late.

There are many ways to interpret phases such as this, and Shirelle would lead me to some later. But for now, no tail-wagger could dissuade me from reaching the worst possible conclusion: I had strived so hard to develop my skills, but had only achieved the ability to create good products no one wanted. There was no point in trying anymore.

Twenty years of struggle had finally given me the self-definition I'd always sought. I now called myself a failure.

The dream was over.

Now what?

Part Three:

How to Battle Negativity

Chapter Eleven:
Learning to Hear

I had no idea what to do, where to turn. I got work substitute teaching at elementary schools, but, while I loved working with the children, I didn't mesh with the necessary regimentation in the job. I wanted to free them, help them express themselves and access their joy, not drill them to stand in line. I was paid to be their trainer, while I wanted to be their Shirelle.

I also took a job at a group home for developmentally disabled men. It offered no future, but it did let me bring Shirelle along, eliciting greetings like, "Doug! I didn't know she was here! I mean, I didn't know!" or, "Good boy! Good boy!" (no matter how many times I corrected the gender) or, "Shirelle! Oh! Would you please!"

So, depressed, directionless, for a year and a half, my life went on hold. No matter what I pursued, I had lost my motivated core. I dated, but whether it was one who berated me for her standing me up, or one who lovingly hung a stocking for Shirelle over her fireplace, all left the same feeling of lack. A lack inside me, not them.

While Shirelle's glorious embrace of life became, not a valued teaching, but a constant insult, reminding me of what my failure rendered impossible in my mind.

Creativity is like when you have a child that says "Hello" for the first time, and you call up your friend or relative about it.

Average writing, for example, is when you tell about what the kid did. Great writing is when you're doing that and the kid walks up to the phone and says, "Hello, hello, hello!" Writer's block is when you say, "Hi! Listen to this! Come on, say hello!" and the kid goes silent and hides. The judgmental gaze that silences the spontaneous voice.

Look at her jump. How beautiful, how full. How she chases the ball. She doesn't compare her jumping or chasing to others. Therefore she can't be a failure or a success.

I was stuck, wishing or waiting for inspiration, while she was always open to it, while going about investigating her world. Certainly she would never opt to wait; she'd whine and tremble herself nuts whenever ordered to hold back. Her ethos was, "Have your pleasure receptors open, and act accordingly!"

How much more I could have created if I'd had her mindset. And it wasn't just me. I saw this problem everywhere. Actors afraid to act, musicians afraid to dare performing. My mother is a very talented painter, though she has only painted two pieces in my lifetime, both on vacations, away from the forces that stifle her best instincts.

Of course, Shirelle wasn't working at some higher level of awareness. It's just that dogs don't have our sense of time. A dog never wonders, "Have I done that yet today?" They learn rules, of nature or of man. But, within those rules, their small brains allow freedom we can only fantasize. An unexamined life so worth living.

So get away from me, Shirelle. Stop rubbing it in.

Another Fourth of July, another parade. We have to wait by the big float truck. I don't want to be there; I'm hot and thirsty and just wish it would end. She's being awful, pulling against me whatever I do, barking at everything. She walks under the truck, though I tell her not to. And after a bit, the truck starts to move. Part of me hopes it'll run over her foot, so she learns to *listen!*

The performers on top scream, the truck stops, and she crawls out, fine.

Wait. Did I really think that? Did I really have a moment of hoping she'd get hurt? How is that possible?

Part of me was resenting her self-centered, greedy childishness. While the other side has always said she's the sweetest, kindest, biggest-hearted...

Both were true, but my fawning said there wasn't a selfish bone in her body, when of course she's very much so. But clearly, there was a darkness in me, too. One that, right now, was reaching a level I couldn't believe: I *felt* that towards her! That wasn't some fictional villain, that was *me!*

Psychologists argue that this shadow-self comes out in such passive ways only when unacceptable feelings are not allowed to express themselves normally. So we'd all be better off if they were more conscious. "But what does that mean? I should treat her badly? Abuse her? In hopes of being more honest, become a detestable jerk?"

It's a balancing act, they say – accept your true consciousness fully, and without judgment, but behave kindly when you can.

"May I see a model? Someone who does it well?"

Of course. As always, look at Shirelle. She manages it. Selfish, but without any smug entitlement or cruelty. Never detestable.

If Shirelle were in a fancy restaurant, she might climb onto someone's table and eat their food, but she would never, ever, insult the waiter.

*

89

The Hiding Place got one last chance. AMC Theaters in Kansas City chose it to test out a self-distribution program, thinking the movie's quality and my hometown-kid status could sell it. For three months, they gave it everything they could, while I worked on publicity full-time – and for a week there I lived a fantasy, with speaking engagements, radio and TV interviews, newspaper stories, all the trappings of the success I'd sought for so long. But in the end, the box-office only recouped their investment. It wasn't a flop, but it also wasn't successful enough to merit their taking it to other markets.

Again, a more positive mindset, like Shirelle's, might have read this experience in a different way. But to me, I was flatlined again, a failure who had just wasted yet more time on a dead wish.

*

She was cute on the phone, cuter in person, and I loved her work. We went out a couple of times, and although she was very hesitant, I wondered if she could pull me out of this funk. Only problem was that she said she was a bit scared of dogs. I thought I'd better try this out before we got attached at all. Took her on a hike, driving in separate cars, so she wouldn't have Bone-Brain sniffing and licking her ear from the back seat.

When we got there, Shirelle jumped up to give her a greeting kiss, and she pulled back, her eyes red and tearing, saying she needed a second to breathe. Then on the hike, she was revolted when Shirelle peed on a bush. After the long hot walk, I took her to a Baskin-Robbins. Over ice cream, I asked how she felt.

"Well, it was a great hike. We would have had more fun, though, if you hadn't brought the dog. You were right, she's very nice, and she behaved herself well. But... she's still a dog."

"Oh, she's a dog and a half. Not a dog for people who don't love dogs."

"Yeah." She hugged me goodbye, and left. Clearly this would be our last date.

Wow, I loved that! Someone who knows who and what she is. Her birthday was the next day and I wrote her a song about the walk and her feelings toward Shirelle and left it on her voicemail.

It would take a couple of months, but that song would bring her back, willing to dare Shirelle again. But somewhere deep inside, Poophead wasn't about to let it be that easy. On a tense morning, as we were finding out just how deep our differences went, Shirelle saw her drive up to my house, pulled from my grasp, and leapt into her open car window and lap, to traumatized shrieks.

Still we tried. Through wince-moments like Shirelle walking into my kitchen and her reacting in shock: "But she's near the food!"

Why? What in me chose this? What sought difficult people and tried to win them over? What constantly fell in love with those intolerant of the core of my heart?

Did she speak for the part of me that would let Shirelle be run over, proof that I really wanted to get rid of the dog? Or did she just fill a reverse place in my psyche, an "equal and opposite reaction" to my overwhelming love for the beast?

She said she was all about boundaries, while I wasn't. Of course not – my idol had been Shirelle for nine years. The tornado of pure love. And both Shirelle and the me that admired her frightened this woman.

But ironically this got me to start building boundaries. To protect her *and* Shirelle. From each other – and perhaps, in some sense, from the negative in me.

*

She had been at her sister's, where her nieces were struck down by a grotesque flu. Related to me the nightmarish house, reeking of vomit, carpets stained. I got all sentimental and talked about how I prayed for the day I could have to clean up after such beloved angels.

Some prayers get answered: That night, Shirelle barfed on my bedspread.

*

And it came to pass that I agreed to a compromise. I loved being greeted every day by Shirelle running and jumping onto me – a joyous splash, like a fresh breeze in the face or a perfect martini – but I knew that many others couldn't stand it. And this relationship seemed to rest on this question: If she felt safe with Shirelle, might she stay?

I found a trainer who specialized in "ADD dogs." We worked with Shirelle, eliciting the expected confusion and re-programming dozings. And got it worked out, with one remaining need: For a while, when guests – especially this one – approached her, they should be armed with a squirt bottle of water, and if she ran at them, shoot her right in the face with it.

"You're coming over? Great! I'll leave the gate open. The bottle's right there."

"Hey Shirelle! Look who's here! That's right, go say hi!"

Each squirt pierced like an icicle into my heart. I'd trained her before, punished her, but this was her best quality, her joyful embrace. Shot down, point blank, right between the eyes.

But it did work. She learned, and began greeting people with sniffs of shoes instead of linebacker slams.

And, as was so often the case, her genius showed up, too. She learned to follow this rule, but also to jump up on anyone who invited her to by slapping his thighs. Which I then did. Every day.

And the romance? How naïve of me to dream that something as puny as a jumping dog could bridge the difference between marriage and impossibility. The obstacles in the relationship just changed from Shirelle to twenty of our other differences.

And once again, I found myself thankful I'd held onto the right one.

In each of these battles with my own negativity, I would beat myself up for not listening to the voice in my head that knew better: Don't write trying to please others, don't toss away who you are to try to make a relationship last, etc. And one night, beating myself up even worse for my wallet having been stolen that day, that inner voice started speaking again, with such firmness that I realized it wasn't exactly mine.

What? It wasn't *mine*? Whose was it then? That voice I would so often ignore. In Grand Junction, "You're driving too fast." In church, "You're not enough to save that woman you love."

I wasn't sure, but the image that came to me was a woman. Sort of like the Blue Fairy in *Pinocchio*. Now I don't personally know any Blue Fairies, so who did that image represent? Much as others might see God as a bearded man, or Love as a nude on a half-shell? Who was it really?

I finally did get a bit of sleep, but woke an hour before my alarm went off. I showered, dressed, and was ready to leave for work…

And there was that face. That beautiful face. Staring at me. Disappointed to see me go. But also caring, knowing I'd had a bad night. As if she were saying to drive carefully.

Her? Shirelle?

I'd been directed to do things before (like to get a dog), but hadn't all these warning voices been since 1994? I'd called her my Guardian Angel for years, but…

As I'd always striven to protect her, had she been working to keep me safe this whole time?

Just how powerful was this creature? And how wise? Could she teach me what I needed to learn about myself, or even about the world as a whole?

Chapter Twelve:
In the World

America has always been a nation of contradictions: Puritanism and religious freedom. All are equal, except blacks, natives, Chinese, women, gays...

On a more subtle level, for all our genius, there's our often-blind love affair with simplicity. A healthy distrust of cold intellectuality led us to rebel against monarchy, and later disagree with Nazi pseudoscience. But in its place, we honor ignorance. When Ronald Reagan said he "forgot" he'd sold arms to anti-American terrorists, it was largely laughed off by the country because he showed folksy character. How frequently do we hear someone brag about not knowing a name, a fact, a song, as though ignorance is a virtue?

Literary critics often argue that the two 'Great American Novels' are *Huckleberry Finn* and *Moby-Dick*. One has as its central character a poor uneducated boy, through whose eyes we see the corruption and hypocrisy of the adult and sophisticated. In the other, an innocent voice describes the danger of megalomania and obsession. Again, this is the greatness of our culture.

By the time Shirelle came along, however, respect for being "dumb and dumber" had reached new heights, championing Bart Simpson's motto: "Underachiever and Proud Of It." When the movie *Forrest Gump* garnered astounding success, many pundits argued for its values, opining that Forrest showed moral character lacking in much of our country. But while no one could deny his goodness, weren't they really honoring Gump's mental lack? Isn't there something in us that looks at a dumb good man and sees him as more moral than a smart complex one? Isn't this dangerous?

Looking to an animal for guidance could lead one down a similar path. Except for one thing: Shirelle never *chose* ignorance. For the things she wanted, she used every bit of her brain. Chasing squirrels, climbing fences, obeying rules – in all, she did her best. She never felt she'd sniffed enough of the neighborhood, or the world.

At times, her heart would lead her to ignore her brain (such as by chasing a cat across a street). That wasn't virtue; it was stupidity. And for that, she needed my protection.

The lesson is subtle but strong. To listen to our hearts as much as she, that would be grace. But not to listen equally to our minds, and remain curious and alert – that leaves us even dumber than that dog running in front of a car. And far more lethal.

*

A second-grade teacher I'd worked for and befriended called me the first day of the new school year. I'd loved her previous class and looked forward to the new one. "I have a student with your favorite name."

"What? You got *another* Boris?"

"No, a name you love even more than that."

A long pause. "Ygor?"

"You're getting warmer."

"You don't mean…"

A couple of weeks later, she took a day off, and had me sub. When the kids finished their morning work, and had a few minutes before recess, I put a Hangman on the board, and said the solution was my dog's name, about which there was something special. They got it just as the bell rang, and the little girl blushed in spotlight amazement.

But during the recess, she walked up to me hurt and sad. Some of her schoolmates had been making fun of her, calling her "Dog-Girl."

When the class came back in, I took the podium. "There seems to have been some confusion. I love my dog more than anything in the world. I think she's the most beautiful thing ever. That's why I gave her the most beautiful name I ever heard."

Problem solved.

It was spelled differently. Her family was Israeli, and her mother had crafted her name, Shirel, from two Hebrew words, to mean "Song of God."

Wow, it really was the same name, wasn't it?

*

Dogs don't know how to lie, though sometimes people think they do. "You're telling me you haven't been fed, but I fed you an hour ago." No – the dog's saying, "I really would like some food," which is true; what happened an hour ago is your concern.

They may be held back from their full truth – say, they want to bark, but they've been trained not to. But that's not lying, just obeying.

How often is that true of us? We learn when we're young that lying is bad, but we also learn politeness. Later this reaches deeper levels: "Don't tell your date you're losing interest in her, because that wouldn't be nice." So she lets her heart take wing, and you later devastate her when you break things off. "Don't tell anyone you think the kid at the next desk is crazy for the things he says and draws; that'd be snitching." So he shows up to school with a semiautomatic and you lose your best friend.

Of course, etymologically, "politeness" is close to "politics," where we see lying every day – though it's considered impolite for one politician to call another a liar. "Misleading" and "mistaken" are the words they use. They're lies, too.

You see, here's the bitter fact about dogs. We can trust them in ways we can't trust other people, because we know they can't lie. And they love and trust us equally, because they don't understand that we can.

It is a beautiful pact, based in the most awful truth about us.

*

Of all the beliefs I developed with Shirelle, the craziest-sounding must be the way we could talk, even beyond the "Blue Fairy" voice. But it did happen.

I talk to myself, lots. And at times I would ask a question out loud. And some of these times, she'd be looking right at me when I'd ask it, and, with a little lick, seem to answer. Not a question like, "What's 349 times 7?" but like, "Are she and I ever going to get back together?" Or I'd ask questions about her, such as, "Are you feeling bad tonight?" And slowly I started suspecting that, when she licked, the answer might be Yes. I tried interpreting the licks that way, and found I was almost always right to do so. Then, if I asked such a question and she stared at me and did nothing, I learned to interpret her answer as No. Or, of course, as that she had no idea what I was asking. That was the tough part; there was no difference between the responses to those two.

"Am I going to get over this?" "Are you doing okay?" "Should I risk it?"

She was like a Magic 8-Ball, but one who only could answer Yes, or nothing.

*

Dogs are bigots.

Shirelle treated different people in different ways, based on whatever prejudices she had. It only elicited apology, never catastrophe, whereas Wolfgang, my childhood dog, possibly unleashed the attack that sealed his doom because of some fatal prejudgment.

Racism is natural; all prejudices are. Prejudice comes from our logical brain, which, for survival, teaches us to make snap judgments about things, based on experience or guidance. Maybe a smart prejudice (beware of big guys in loose masks carrying chainsaws), maybe a really stupid one (women can't lead).

Dogs have logical brains. So they make judgments based on their experience, too.

I was walking Shirelle once, when a beautiful friendly Newfoundland approached us. Shirelle had never backed down to any dog (or horse, car, or anything else), but she fell onto her back at once, completely submissive, terrified.

It was about Annie – the dog who'd attacked her as a puppy. Similar hair, shape, features. And about as much bigger than her as Annie had been then. To her eyes, this Newfoundland *was* Annie. While she generally lived without fear, this memory was perfect enough to terrify her.

This supplication was from a form of racial prejudice. Maybe Wolfgang's attack on our mailman was, too; maybe a black man had hurt him once before. Whatever it was, I'm sure his reaction was founded in some reason.

An adequate reason. For someone with a dog-sized brain.

We have to do better. To make judgments more worthy than a dog's, we must use the higher parts of our brains to overcome our raw survivalist logic. To look honestly at our fears, and the reasons behind them, to opt for the best actions.

Without acknowledging what's right in our prejudices, we end up victims of chainsaw murders. But without looking beyond them, we can be victimized by ourselves.

For example, some time after we agreed to send our armies to retaliate for an unconscionable attack on our buildings, planes, and citizens, we came to realize that one of the countries our leaders chose to invade had nothing to do with those attacks. Its leadership were mortal enemies of the hijackers' cabal. Removing them only helped those who had created the atrocity.

So why had the American people been behind the Iraq invasion? Simple – we were sure we knew all about Arab Muslims. We'd seen what they could do.

And since we *knew* they were all the same, and all worked together with the same morals and desires, we *knew* the solution to our problem was to hit them all with "Shock and Awe." Just as Wolfgang *knew* to attack the mailman.

Dogs are blameless for such acts. Their brains don't have the potential for higher thought. But, for such sins of ignorance, we are deeply, fatally, guilty.

*

Whether it was because I've finally gained the mindset to hear it, or because the information is simply new, a light softly ignites in the tomb of my dead career. An expert on entertainment professionals tells me about MFT, or Marriage and Family Therapist, a license for psychotherapists that only takes two years of study, giving me the ability to make my own hours – to write, direct, and maybe even have a life. Besides, male therapists who want to focus on children are in great demand. She recommends a few schools. The best is near my home.

I visit, I love it, I apply, I'm accepted. It's one day a week, so I can still teach to pay bills. While Shirelle spends my school day teaching neighbors' children to enjoy having a dog in their yard, so they can get their own someday.

I dive in. Embrace re-definition. I'm still me, but without the promise I'd fought for two decades for, or its draining fear and embarrassment.

My soul was returning. I was defining myself anew, and in renewed love with that dog. The questions I'd had – of what I'd felt toward her – now shone as patently absurd, brought on by my core having been so crushed by other parts of my life. I would face many disappointments in the future, but I would never question my feelings for her again.

How ironic that it had been in this uninvited swamp of negativity that my ability to learn from her, to perceive her lessons, had so escalated. The worst of times, yes, but necessary.

I had learned how to learn from Shirelle. And there was only one her. But you can do it too, in your world. Anyone can. It's all about focus. Obsessive focus, though. And you have to really mean it; it has to come from love.

Try it. Write down a list of the ten things you'd most like to change about yourself – five if you're cocky. And then let your mind go to the thing you love most, to see how it deals with those concepts. No, not your spouse or parent or kid; that's a different kind of love, too complex a relationship. What can you love purely? Marcel Proust used a certain cookie, and Ray Bradbury dandelion wine, to travel into reveries about their pasts. Thoreau loved a pond through which he created an entire worldview.

What are you just crazy about? What seems perfect to you? Maybe a flower? What can that flower tell you about yourself? How to grow? How to bloom, shine, attract, show off? How to fade away? Altogether, how to live?

But don't stop there. Keep it going. If the love is real, you'll never tire of it. What do you see in that thing today? It'll be different tomorrow. A new lesson, a new awareness. How would it deal with the problems you're facing if it were in your shoes?

Look. You'll find answers.

People put down "looking through the eyes of love" as a blindness. But in the right context, it is a phenomenal key to finding one's truth.

*

Was this the most beautiful hike yet? Places where the woods were so burnt out that nothing was growing, others where the fire had never hit and all was lush. And everything in between. Wildflowers that only appear right after a burn, just to be evolutionarily beaten by others, though the seeds survive for next time. Stringy upright things that look like Dr. Seuss. Brilliant hues, and areas lacking all color, which, late afternoon after rains, might look desolate, or shimmer in glowing black and silver. And suddenly a meadow, untouched.

And a blur of orange and white throughout, making me feel so high. My drug of choice – this speed, this ecstasy, this dope!

*

I'm filling my tank. Her head is out the car window, gazing at me. The gas station's radio suaves out Lou Rawls' "You'll Never Find Another Love Like Mine."

Indeed darling. And backatcha.

Chapter Thirteen:
Who We Are

I see you flat out on the floor
I hear your soft contented snore
I've learned so much from books I've read
But not what goes on in your head.

How does your mind work?
What do you see?
What goes through you?
Do you feel yourself be?

What do you think of the jingle of your collar
What do you think of eating from your bowl
What do you think of our home when I'm not with you
Is a tree to you the same as a telephone pole?

What am I to you?

What are you to you?

What is everything that's true to you?

What I would give to know what you've reckoned

To feel your consciousness, just for a second.

To feel yourself, to be yourself

To know if it's actually true

To just know how you see yourself

To know the perfection

Of you past connection

To live the complete purity of you.

*

    I threw a party for Shirelle's tenth birthday. Barbecue, good friends, their kids, and their dogs. I asked people to come as their role models, so I dressed as Shirelle: orange pants and button-down shirt, white t-shirt, a tail made out of coat hangers and construction paper, an orange cap, and an old collar of hers.

    A lot of people brought gifts and treats. My friends Kevin and Kathryn wrote on their card "Ten More Years!" summarizing all I was feeling.

    And she was fine now. Perfect, really. She didn't need any more training. She never chewed anymore, or wandered, would obey my orders when she barked (Not to say she wasn't still capable of surprises – like the time I stepped out of the shower just in time for her to drop a freshly-caught squirrel at my feet).

Yet I still lived in perpetual fear of something bad happening to her. My life now had no goal nearly as high as keeping her safe.

So, daily, I would tell her, upon leaving, "Just one rule: Don't break my heart."

*

I'd had no desire to go back to school, but I adored it once there. And with each step my life improved, I saw better the blocks that had held me back. And how my sweet companion had worked on me, in so many ways. How her way of relating modeled Carl Rogers' concept of holding clients in a state of Genuineness and Unconditional Positive Regard; how she fit, in my mind, nearly every Jungian archetype; even questioning whether watching her tail wag affected the neurons in my brain in the same way eye-movement treatments do. As a therapist, Shirelle had proven pretty perfect for me.

Meanwhile, I kept hearing talk about animal-assisted therapy. How healing it can be to have a dog or a cat in the room (or even outdoor sessions with a horse). Made sense. But given how some people were put off by Shirelle's ebullience, I figured she wasn't eligible. Plus, in order for me to advertise her, she'd have to be tested and approved, which seemed too much work.

What I didn't realize was that she had one big lesson in Psychology still to teach me. The biggest.

Right before an experience that would turn both our lives upside down forever.

But first, that lesson.

*

It was Christmastime, and while all this work was heading me in the right direction, I still felt ridiculous – still single, still without a legitimate career yet. I had no desire to visit my family in this condition, but nowhere else to go for the holidays.

I had been buried in my work – as a student, as a part-time teacher, and as a trainee therapist, working with kids again. The work came surprisingly naturally to me, with the necessary tools of listening, encouraging, using humor, initiating play, and building self-worth, all an easy translation of my Knucklehead-ology of the previous decade. My greatest flaw (and strength) was that I cared too much, got too attached, and was too eager to help out in ways beyond my "scope of practice." To the point that, one day, a supervisor blasted me with definition: "Doug, you are a Golden Retriever." Close, very close.

As such, I thought about these clients all the time. For instance… This beautiful teen, an overachiever in athletics, academics, social life. Kind, considerate. What's not to like, not to offer unending pride to her parents? But they would criticize her looks, her weight. I had dealt with body dysmorphias, such as people seeing themselves as heavier than they are. But how could one's whole family have that problem?

Waiting in the airport, overhearing conversations. One couple discussing how they were going to deal with a stupid in-law at a holiday dinner. A woman presented with a gift by a child, faking how pleased she was with it, and the kid faking believing her. Another couple, walking together but their uptight dismissal of each other exuding from every pore. Not just anger, but embarrassment. Why were they like this?

I walked away to look at magazines. No escape there – the covers all selling inhuman skinniness for women or pneumatic chests for men. And the gossip. What this celebrity got caught doing, what one said about another.

All irritating. I just wanted to go back home and be with Shirelle, who never was so boring.

I boarded the plane and we accelerated into the sky. I looked out the window as we rose above the smog of L.A. It's not so bad in the winter, but it's still there, and you can especially see it when you get above it.

I thought of my first day as an undergrad, the Introductory Sociology teacher greeting us with, "If fish were anthropologists, the last thing they'd discover would be water." I wondered when we'd really discover what we'd been breathing.

I got to Kansas City, still negative. With no little children believing in Santa, my family's gift exchanges had become a chore, purchases to meet the tastes of kin we hadn't lived with in decades.

Hyper-sensitized, I bristled at hearing jabs, complaints, all around us – and from us. As if everyone were that girl's relatives insulting her.

By Christmas morning, I was laser-focused on every word that might fit that category, to argue my case. Every jovial crack, every hint of deficiency. And every word I heard seemed to almost be shaming enough.

Every word.

And something clicked in me.

Every word held it. Not just insults, but compliments too. And so did asking for another egg, or more coffee – as though it were a language of its own. Negative, accusing, assuming the worst always. Every word.

Again that Sociology teacher's line came to me. "The last thing they'd discover." The thing. What Shirelle must see every day, especially in me. The last thing *I'd* discover. What was in my air, my family's air, maybe everyone's air. Our Air, our Water, our Fire and Earth.

And I began to create, or rather to see for the first time, a world-view, horrific in its implication, that explained so much of my journey. And put Shirelle's importance in my life yet higher.

Sit back. This gets complex.

*

It starts with the concept of how one deals with the consequences of breaking rules.

When one obeys the rules, and does what's expected, the world can't see anything about that person's true personality. But when one breaks rules, goes outside accepted boundaries, even by mistake, their truth is revealed.

If someone does something defined as bad, there are six possible feelings they might experience as a result.

As an example, let's say a man accidentally runs a red light. He might experience:

Apathy: He doesn't care. He feels no regret, doesn't feel bad about it at all. Nor does the fact that he did it affect how he sees himself. He ran the light, maybe didn't hit anyone, maybe didn't get caught, so he sees no problem.

Self-Doubt: He's aware of what he did, and that fact makes him aware that he potentially could do it again. He might "wake up" to the fact that he's not paying enough attention to his driving. It's a change in self-concept, but not self-worth.

Regret/Remorse: From mild Regret to full Remorse, this is a sincere sorrow at the effects of one's actions. Say he ran the red light and hit another car, injuring the driver, and feels ill about it. This may even entail empathy, in which he feels that other driver's physical pain.

Guilt: He acknowledges that what he did was "wrong," morally incorrect. In our legal system, Guilt is assuaged by paying fines or jail time; in the Catholic Church, it is done so through confession; in Judaism through atonement. A person

110

can feel Guilt without remorse, or any long-term change in self-image. He runs the light, admits to the arresting officer that he did it, tells his priest that he did it, and after paying whatever restitution they say he must, feels fine.

Pride: He recognizes the abnormality of what he did, and feels good about it. Maybe he likes having broken a rule in running that light. Or maybe he's perversely proud of scaring or hitting a person. Either way, it produces a positive charge.

Shame: He sees what he's done, and it pulls him into a negative view of himself. While Shame may be instigated by Remorse, Guilt, or a mixture of the two, it is different from them in that it centers on *overall self-definition*. Instead of self-doubt, which is specific to the cause, Shame blurs boundaries, creating a universal belief: "I ran that red light and hit a car, therefore I am irresponsible, stupid, and unworthy of respect."

(A couple of notes about this list: First, only one of these six categories completely lacks an emotional component: Self-Doubt. One can experience Self-Doubt with any emotion, or none. Second, some argue that there's another reaction, Denial. The guy could convince himself he *didn't* run that light. But I'd argue that at least one of these reactions had to come first, before he talked himself out of the truth.)

Now think of all this in terms of Shirelle. Most of these reactions involve some act of judgment. But while judgment was far rarer in her than in a human, she still did experience five of these six:

Apathy: Shirelle would go ballistic at dogs or people passing by – for example, a uniformed meter-reader – and relax fully the second they were out of sight. I imagined her smilingly shrugging to me, "There's just something about a man in uniform." He was gone, she was fine, no feelings about it at all.

Self-Doubt: This showed most clearly in the training incidents I've mentioned, when she would struggle with her inability to understand the punishment/reward consequences of her actions, until she'd had time to mull it over.

Regret/Remorse: Shirelle showed me total Remorse twice in her life:

Once because she, in the middle of a mad bark at a neighbor, knocked a plant down, breaking it and shattering dirt over a rug. And when I walked in and saw it and yelled "oh *No!*" she fell. Her eyes squeezed shut, her head bowed, her legs collapsed, all pulled in.

She hit hard, I saw it, and my heart broke with her. "It's okay, it's just dirt, a pot, it'll be all right." Such kindness in her, to feel so bad about this.

The other time, in playing tug-of-war, she bit Dawn's hand. Dawn pulled back, "Ow!" and down Shirelle went. The same expression, the same devastation. If human, she would have been sobbing. "Not Dawn! I love Dawn! Did I really bite her?! Dawn, who loves me? Who visits? Who plays with me? Who calls me Squash-Head? I've broken life's vow, all is lost!"

But no, it wasn't. Because Dawn saw, and melted too, and loved that dog more than ever before.

True Remorse is the ultimate beauty in pain. And all in its presence must stand back in awe. And forgive, with nothing held back. So easily.

Pride: Visitors would stay over, sleeping on my roll-out sofa. I'd keep Shirelle in my room with me overnight, but when I let her out in the morning, she would run and scud herself onto the couch, her freezing nose instantly inserted into the warmest sleeping flesh. Then once she'd awakened the poor soul, she'd plant herself firmly onto their bed, granting them love, but not a lot of room. Chest out, proud of all she had done. The more frustrated they were, the better.

Guilt: Just as with people, her Guilt wasn't a very deep-seated emotion. She'd disobey me when I called her, or take food she knew wasn't hers, and accept the berating that ensued. Rarely did she give the impression that the Guilt wasn't worth the crime.

But never, not once, did she show Shame.

It wasn't just because she was a dog. Ygor had been loaded with neurotic Shame, always doubting his acceptability, at least to others. But not Shirelle. Never did she decide she was a bad or unworthy being.

*

Sometimes we hear of people complimented for lacking Self-Doubt: That lack is said to be a necessary component of heroism, fortitude. Now of course no one, outside of the fully delusional, lacks it completely, but for self-protection, a person who has done something wrong might say they lack it.

(For example, when the second President Bush was asked what mistakes he had made in invading Iraq, he strategically responded that he had made none. Acknowledging Self-Doubt would have raised the question of what emotion he then felt about it – Apathy, Remorse, Guilt, Pride, or Shame. And to admit any of those would have revealed a dark truth that would have destroyed him politically.)

What we really want to admire is someone who can experience Self-Doubt without descending into Shame. This is difficult. Shame is as uncontrollable as cancer and as overwhelming and destructive as any mood-altering drug.

And once let in, Shame fills its victim's head with screaming voices of disdain, such that they can't even find their own true voice. And even the simplest pleasure in life – the doing of good – becomes lost. Because Shame, such a liar, barricades one from full empathy.

While Shirelle, who somehow lacked Shame, greeted the world with unmitigated love every day.

*

Now all this bad feeling makes sense, if one has done something truly so awful as to ruin their own self-image. But as I sat with my family on this celebratory morning, I saw no one bearing any such crime. So what was the reason for this?

It's not quite air, because it's not outside us – it's part of us. I can't say it's our blood, because it's not natural, and can't be extracted. It's a personality, but it is learned. It's a culture, but not in any conscious way. It's something absorbed so fundamentally that we're completely unaware of it. And it's at the core of our communication, with others and ourselves.

It went back to that thought I'd had about Shirelle's mind long ago, about Language: I speak and hear The Language of Shame.

More intrinsic to my communication than English ever was. And this was no more created by one person or a few than English had been. No one in that room was intending to speak in Shame, but not one word avoided it. Shame had pervaded every molecule of my life, our lives.

Do all humans speak this language, breathe this air? Is it endemic to self-awareness? Is it the Curse of Eden, that along with mortality and wanting to cover up our private parts, we're destined to confront Shame at all times and in all things? Doesn't the great majority of advertising and marketing rely on our feeling "not enough?" Don't most of us spend our lives working to overcome that feeling – or giving up? Yet I, and those close to me, seemed more mired in it than others, who might churn in a Language of Guilt and Blame, or even Abuse.

I examined this group in front of me. I had never felt as separate from them, but too had never felt such love for them. The Shame that had filled me throughout my life, I realized, could not be cured or ridded by them. Nor by anyone I'd been drawn to. Because every one of these people spoke the same language. Henry Higgins could improve Eliza's proper grammar, but no teacher could have taught her to forget English as a whole.

My mind raced.

The cruelest thing about Shame is that it causes one to value falsely: The victim puts more trust in things and people they don't really believe in than those they do, and distrusts what feels right. Because of this, Shame-based people raise their children in the Language of Shame, though they'd never consciously wish that pain on them.

My parents had been brought up by wonderful people, who had been deeply shaming. And it was easy to find things in my grandparents' childhoods that made them feel shamed, if it wasn't in them already.

So the Shame-speaker, by definition, is naturally drawn toward those who share his Language, or finds the "multilingual" but speaks only the Shame Language to them. How else can one carry on a conversation? Ergo my bad relationships. How many times in my life had my acts hurt others, or had others hurt me, not because of desire to do so, but simply due to being mired in Shame?

My mind kept racing, like a dying man's flashing over the events of his life.

There was every girlfriend – their beauty and their flaws and their warmth and their humor and their mystery – and me dealing with them in the Language of Shame. In prayerful hope one of them could free me from its ongoing crushing of my soul.

My lack of sustained success in the film business – oh, how a less shamed filmmaker would have parlayed my movie's acclaim into a deal!

Friends – those I'd lost and those I'd kept, all of us mired in Shame, one way or another.

My writers' block. What better example of The Language of Shame could I have had? I face what I wrote the day before, or what's just going through my mind at that moment, and denigrate it, put it down, say it can't work. Every precious idea shoved through this most destructive of filters.

And even my theater productions. The gifts of applause the *only* moments when I'd felt validated. But did I then absorb, like Sally Field's Oscar speech, that, "You really like me?" No, it was only, "For this moment, for this short burst of time, thank you for freeing me from the pain of my unending Shame."

And the play always closes. Or is rejected. Or the romance doesn't work out. Or the movie is not picked up. And years of work, and all inspiration, conspire to label Failure. Failure not just to make a living, but to earn an excuse to live. Failure to move past the Shame.

Meanwhile, I was still in this room. This room, with this family. They had *loved* my movies, plays, and videos. Why? Because those were *their* stories. These people got it, got me. For my stories were tales of Shame. I felt so close to them, knowing this secret I so wanted to tell them, and realizing there was no way I could possibly express it at that moment.

That must be what Shirelle felt toward me all the time.

*

I sat in the airport later, thinking about what it would be like to fly home to yet another Christmas night without a girlfriend.

But there was a freedom I could feel as well. I looked around me at the other passengers, reading books, listening to music, watching cable news. All looking for answers. Isn't that human history, the search for answers? How often has someone said they'd found The Answer? How often have others agreed that that someone was right?

But the only answer I had was that I didn't have any answers at all. If one speaks the Language of Shame, breathes the air of Shame, there can be no answers. For how can one feel the beauty of boundless faith, the clarity of cold atheistic life-in-the-moment, the security of committed intimacy, the excitement of serial romance, the comfort of membership, the strength of solitude, the peace of anonymity, the thrill of fame, the Zen of freedom from ownership, or the bounty of wealth and power – if one can't feel their own *worth*? And Shame will always prevent that feeling.

What could life be, if I could figure how to remove that obstacle? Sports are a lot easier if you're not drunk; music sounds better without static. How much better could life's pursuits be in the cleaner air of non-Shame? To hear it when it comes, but refuse to grant it power. To feel anything else – fury, pain, insult, fear of death, fear of anything – but not descend into Shame. But how could I do so?

I had no idea.

But I was sure of one thing. When I got home, no matter what was on the answering machine, or the email, or being yelled at me from inside my own head – no matter what, I would be with a force who would greet me with no Shame, because she lived free of it.

I boarded the airplane, and we left the earth and broke through the clouds.

*

The Persian poet Rumi talks about how every millisecond is new. Everything is rebirth.

I think that's the way dogs live. They get bored if they're caged up. But it's sure exciting when something walks down the street.

If you can look at life that way, and live that every second is new, it's the opposite of saying, "I had her, but she's gone." It's "What's this next second?" Every moment is the opening chord of a song we've never heard.

My dad once asked me, "Aren't there are only a few truly great songs?" And I retorted, "I don't choose to live that way." Kind of snotty, but I think I was right. I might hear the best song ever for the first time tomorrow, if I let myself.

You can say that about everything. Shirelle never figured today would be less than yesterday.

As usual, how right she would prove to be.

Part Four:

The Spotlight

Chapter Fourteen:
The Insidious

Ill winds blow. How long did it take me to learn this? Some say it's due to planets, others more theological reasons. But it does happen. Strange things occur – people are meaner, more traffic accidents occur, everyone's tense… and our lives change. New loves walk in, others leave, births, deaths – and when it's over, whether the changes are seen as good or bad, we breathe sighs of relief that these winds of change have eased. For as long as they're blowing, whether consciously or unconsciously, we know nothing is secure, and everything we hold dear is suddenly vulnerable.

*

A month after I graduated the psychology school, I was a ball of stress. I still required a summer course in order for my diploma to count, I had a backlog of work to do at home, even the traffic was particularly insane. But I was focused on something else.

When Shirelle had been almost a year old, I read a review of a new play. The concept was terrific: the triangle between a man, his wife, and their dog, with the dog played by a sexy young woman. The descriptions of the dog's activities and speech sounded hilarious. When it was published, I bought a copy at once. That night I lay on my bed and opened it, and Shirelle jumped up and stretched her whole body along mine. She didn't move till I'd finished it, a magical experience.

I had never seen a dog anthropomorphized in a way I found so true. From her innocent desire to be loved, to her bratty misbehavior, to her wail of Cole Porter's "Ev'ry Time We Say Goodbye" when she's left at home alone, to her full-out obscenities screamed at a cat, to the life-altering impact she has on her bewildered owners, this was Shirelle and me. When I finished it, I knew I had to see this play – *Sylvia* by A. R. Gurney – and, if at all possible, to direct it.

I was working with two theater companies, but neither agreed to do it. One played to a conservative, mostly older audience, and refused the crudeness of Sylvia's behavior when she was in heat, and the language of the aforementioned cat scene. The other, which prided itself on being edgy, wouldn't touch it because of the image of a young woman sitting at the feet of a middle-aged man cooing, "You're my God!"

But one night at my beloved Theatre Palisades, a friend asked if I'd heard that their sister theater was going to be doing *Sylvia* in the fall of 2005, right after I was to graduate. Right when I'd need a break from two years of nonstop academic work.

I'd sworn that I'd never do amateur theater again, but just this once... See, I'd seen the play done, but always felt they missed the key truth in it: Dogs don't think they're cute. They're focused and serious and never do anything halfway. I'd seen cute actresses showing me how cute they thought they were while they faux-yelled cutely at an offstage cat. No, I wanted what I'd seen when I read it. I wanted fire. I wanted a woman to channel the energy of Shirelle's spraining lunges – where cute becomes destructive and uproarious and profound. I wanted that mix of selfishness and loyalty, that playfulness and epic inappropriateness, that Gurney captured as no one else has. I wanted my childhood dogs, and especially my Knucklehead, on that stage. It wouldn't be my grandest production, but it could be the statue I'd always wanted to build to her, and to all of them.

I spent the next year thinking about it. Defining the tone I wanted, staging it in my mind, and, with joyous relish, planning music. At its core, this is a love story, so I didn't want to go for cutesy "dog" songs, but rather to honor the play's romanticism and depth. Harry James' recording of "Skylark" might seem more appropriate for a drama set in the 1940's South. But the call of his trumpet, and the wistfulness of Helen Forrest's wail, made it the perfect opening, expressing the search the lost endure for love (even more so if you're a stray mutt in Central Park); also it made a perfect lead-in to James and Forrest's ode to wartime fidelity, "I Don't Want to Walk Without You," which I sang to Shirelle almost daily. Other pieces came even more out of left field – Leonard Cohen's paean to mysterious lovers "Suzanne;" Stephen Sondheim's ulcerously bewildered "Losing My Mind;" and, to close, John Lennon's childlike, sad "Love" fading into the sparkling vulnerability of George Harrison's "What Is Life." And, as a necessary signature, an intermission inclusion of The Shirelles' "Baby It's You."

At the interviews for the gig, I was up against a fully qualified opponent, but of course won. Who could stand up to the desire and commitment (a.k.a. obsessive insanity) I took into that room? They warned me of technical difficulties, but this wouldn't require much – as long as I could find the cast. And most especially, a girl of supernatural quality, able to embody all I saw in the character of Sylvia.

*

On July 25, Shirelle and I take a long walk, me just thinking about the callbacks tomorrow night. Then that night, when I'm about to head out, she's suddenly lethargic. That's normal in the summer heat, but she doesn't even want a treat. Maybe she's eaten something bad, but I'm in a hurry. I'll see how she is when it's cooler tonight, but I've got to get to dinner. Just to be sure, I look her in the eyes and ask her, and she licks, so I figure it's okay to go.

However, I speed home afterward, and find she can't stand. I pick her up and run her to the local emergency pet hospital, thinking I'd walked her too long, and there's something wrong with her hips. I always knew that'd happen someday.

But it's not her hips. It's internal bleeding.

To the degree that her heart is shrinking from loss of blood.

Her pulse is 170 beats per minute, when 110 is normal.

Her spleen has a tumor, and it's burst and it's shooting blood out.

The tumor could be a number of things, one of which is cancer.

So they need to remove the entire organ, saying she doesn't need it to live. But they can't do it tonight, and it's expensive, so they suggest I might just want to put her down.

What?

I'm dizzy. Not connected to my own air. On autopilot, I tell them no. So she stays overnight with an IV in her leg, so that if anything goes wrong they can put more blood in.

I'll talk to my vet in the morning, and get her take on it.

So I guess, if she really was saying I could go to dinner, Shirelle meant, "It's okay, I'll live?" But then why am I feeling so queasy, and not quite in my own body?

I light a candle in my room for her. All I can think of is the way she normally gallops into vets' offices, jumping up on the counter. And I almost start crying. But I can't. I have to sleep.

After a few hours, I wake to see the little tea candle in its thin metallic container is completely melted, a huge flame about to set my bookshelf on fire. I try to move it, but of course it burns my fingers. How am I going to put it out? I put some water in it and it splashes hot wax everywhere, including up into my face. Good. This flame is Shirelle, and she is *Mad* about being in that hospital, biting at me. She has some fire in her!

126

My vet calls, and says she's "really scared."

She wants me to take Shirelle to another place across town that she thinks is best. I go back to the emergency hospital, and while I wait for them to prepare her, a family walks in to pick up a little white dog they had dropped off when I'd been there the night before. I tell them what's wrong with Shirelle. They say, "Oh, you shouldn't do the surgery; we took our dog to an incredible acupuncturist for a tumor, and he was able to make it go away." I say she'd bleed to death in two days if we didn't operate. But they give me his phone number.

I drive hours to get Shirelle to this other place, and a vet looks at her and finds the same stuff. Says the odds are 70 percent that it's cancerous. "We're going to operate, and when we open her up, we'll see if there are other tumors, and if there are, we'll call you before we proceed, to see what we should do."

And it was only then, at "to see what we should do," that my whole world dropped. Up to then, I'd kept detached in get-what's-necessary-done numbness. Enabling me to do everything for her, without engaging fear of loss.

But when he said those words, that I'd have to make a *decision*, I went cold. My little girl was going to be cut open, she might be full of tumors, and I might have to give the word to put her down. To kill her. To lose her. The sleeping part of me awoke, and silently began screaming.

Life was no longer about deadlines. Life was love and terror.

*

I left her in the hospital and started to make shivering phone calls, asking people to send thoughts or prayers. Nothing else to do. It was too late to cancel the evening's plans, and what good could that do for her anyway? So I went to meet with the set designer to go over ideas, and then have the callback audition, trying to regain my detachment.

During the meeting, my cell phone rang to tell me they were starting the operation. I tried to put my attention onto the set. Anything.

Then the phone rang again. Too soon. The surgeon's number flashed. I knew – it's over, she's gone. I answered it, he said a couple of words, and the signal dropped out.

I ran outside, and tried to call him back, but couldn't get through. A voicemail announced itself. "Just wanted to let you know that Shirelle did fine during surgery, and we're in the process of waking up." He'd called so quickly because it was all a breeze.

It was as good as the news could possibly be, freeing me to do my best through the night, but all I wanted was to walk away and let the play go.

*

Normally I find callback auditions invigorating, and afterwards I'm unable to sleep till I've put the ideal cast together. This time it would take days to focus on something so suddenly unimportant.

Besides seeing how actors interacted, I had a few specific needs, such as to make sure they could sing. But now, having spent a day facing the unthinkable, how was I to watch a bunch of beautiful women pretending to be dogs sing to me, "Every time we say goodbye I die a little?" I'd just check their pitch and range instead.

Sporadically, frantic helplessness would kick in: What am I doing here anyway? Why aren't I with her?

I get to the hospital at midnight. They lead me to her cage in the operating area. She's been gutted like a fish. My heart just falls. She's stoned out on a bunch of IVs, maybe a tenth awake. They open the door for me to pet her, she groggily looks up at me, stands up, "Good. You're here. Let's go." And forthrightly walks out of all the tubes. I and everyone in the room rush to grab her, to get her back in the cage, hook her back up. Drugged and a whisker away from death, but still the Knucklehead.

*

The next morning, she was able to walk on a leash, and a day later, was weak but able to travel. I brought her home. The biopsy results, telling whether the tumor was cancerous or not, would come later.

*

I got the cast together for a first read-through, leaving Shirelle with my visiting niece, to make sure she didn't lick the 35 staples in her belly. It was the only way for her not to have to wear a cone; the miserable thing had such a long nose that she needed the largest kind, which kept her from being able to use her dog-door, and often, in her weakness, would pull her head down in such a way that she couldn't move.

I told the cast about the previous week, eliciting predictable shock. When we got to reading the last scene, where the husband tells the audience about the dog losing her faculties, the actor burst into tears. By the end, the entire cast had.

I told them this would be the focus of the play now.

*

For the next few days, Shirelle quietly healed, only showing misery when I'd leave and have to put the cone on her. Other people were saying they felt positive, that she'd be okay. Then, while I was driving her home from getting treatment from my chiropractor, her surgeon called me. Again, the phone signal went out. I figured that was a good sign. When I got home, I lit candles, sat down on the floor with her, and called the surgeon back to hear the good news.

But it wasn't good news.

They had performed two biopsies. The one on the liver was clean, meaning that the cancer hadn't developed anywhere else. But the spleen tumor was Hemangiosarcoma, what they call an "insidious" cancer, because it grows undetectably inside organs, and then, when big enough, bursts open. It loves the spleen best of all, but its next two favorite organs are the heart and the liver, so this was a death sentence. Chemotherapy might double her life expectancy, though.

A life expectancy that currently was two months.

The second I got off the phone with him, I phoned that acupuncturist, and arranged to see him. And made a firm decision that she would come with me to every rehearsal. I wasn't going to be leaving her alone now.

The echo inside: Two months. What does that mean? Not even to closing night. Should I give this play up?

No. Painful as it might be, I had a responsibility to her. This wasn't going to be just a great comedy anymore, but neither would it be a dirge.

I announced to the cast that I had to undo what I'd told them the first night. If the biopsy had been good, I'd be cheering. But still, this wouldn't be about dying. It would be a celebration of life, the way she lived it. It would be unlike anything I'd ever done. It would be Hers.

I was lost, and hadn't the faintest idea what I was doing. I was frightened to my core. If I could only turn time around, but I couldn't. So I walked, with her, forward, into where all was unknown.

Except for a very good script.

Chapter Fifteen:
Believing

Sylvia tells the story of Greg and Kate, a married couple in New York City, facing life alone together after their kids have left home. Frustrated with his boring job, Greg takes a break in Central Park, where he meets a stray mongrel, and they instantly connect. He brings Sylvia home, and excitedly tells Kate of his wonderful addition to their lives. Kate doesn't want a dog, and sees this lively brat as an intrusion that will keep her from pursuing her own goals, but Greg coaxes her to allow Sylvia to stay temporarily. His relationship with Sylvia deepens, while he begins skipping more work and looking at life in new ways, and Kate gets more and more frustrated. They both commiserate with friends – for Greg, it's a macho guy in the dog park; for Kate, an upper-crust society matron. Eventually, after trying couple's therapy (the manly dude, matron, and therapist all played by the same actor), Kate makes the demand: Sylvia or her. Beaten down but loyal, Greg finds a new home for the dog, but Kate finally realizes that Sylvia is actually saving their marriage, and changes her mind.

Greg and Kate then walk out and tell us that Sylvia stayed with them for eleven years, that their marriage deepened, and that eventually they had to put her down. Greg describes the act in detail, and Kate prods him to show the audience Sylvia's picture. He pulls out a snapshot, and, behind them, a large image of Sylvia is projected onto the set. But it's not the actress we've been watching for two hours;

it's the face of a dog. The light fades on the sad happy couple, brightening on the spirit of the late pooch.

My Greg and Kate, David Burr and Georgan George (I know, what a name!), were lovely souls, both divorcees, so with a sadness beneath their humor that gave just the edge I wanted. For the three-character role, I had a difficult choice between an excellent actor I'd directed twice before and a new one, ending up taking the unknown quantity, Gregory Blair, as his nimble, sharp energy was more what the cast chemistry needed.

I had called eight women back to audition for the part of Sylvia. All would have been fine in the role. But I had an idea, and asked them to *improvise* the scene when she sees the cat. I said to cut loose, not hold anything back, be as awful as possible.

And only one went all the way.

I had been impressed by Wendy Douglas in a musical a few months before, but didn't know if she'd be right for this. In her initial audition, her body work was great, except that it was feline, not a dog at all. I asked her about it, and she admitted she owned a cat, had never had a dog. But then at the callback, she brought a ton of doggy choices, as well as full-on vile hatred of the cat, and a sexuality so rampant I'd have to pull it back. The fact that she was a tall, strong, long-legged redhead, just like Herself, just made the choice even more clear.

*

I took Shirelle to see the acupuncturist. Wordlessly – the man didn't speak English – he put his hands on her head and neck, and stuck three needles in her, and when we walked out she had four times the energy she had had walking in. He said (through his assistant) that his sense was that she had a medium level of cancer in her. Not high, not low.

Friends were wonderful, and sent beautiful thoughts. It's interesting, though, how some people, meaning to be nice, are so quickly negative. "Oh Doug, I'm so sorry, and I understand. I remember when we had to put our dog down…" And I'd stop them, afraid to let bad energy into her.

But good vibes flowed in as well. One friend gave her energy work. Our chiropractor cracked her strength up. And I even got a bell to hang from her collar, made for motorcyclists to dangle from their handlebars, to ward off evil spirits with each ring.

The part of me that had been frozen shut was now ripped wide open. And all that gushed out was love, love beyond even what I'd found before.

*

With each acupuncture session she got better and better. Still slept a lot, but growing back into her old personality – barking at cats, chasing balls and squirrels.

The acupuncture doctor had written a book about Feng Shui, including the idea that beamed ceilings – like those over my bed – interrupt energy flow. That made sense, because my flow had seemed interrupted ever since we'd moved into this house a couple of years before. I turned the bed around, wondering if I'd missed signals Shirelle had given about energies like this. There's stuff in the book about how children will be the first to pick up the good or bad spirit of a place. What about dogs?

On a recommendation from others who believe in such things, I burned sage to clear out any bad spirits. Amazingly, I could *feel* where the trapped energy was. And some hostile energy in places – previous residents of the house with unfinished business, I surmised.

And as I felt the heavy energy subside, I could see Shirelle loving it. Every time I asked her, "Are you liking this?" she'd lick. That soft, chin-on-the-ground, focused-on-me joy.

And as I worked on making the house a better place to be, everything pointed to the same moral: Improve the flow, get rid of the fear, and move into a new day.

*

Meanwhile, the cast of the show was so positive, so hard-working. They made it difficult for me, moving faster than I'd scheduled. But more importantly, they bonded with Shirelle beautifully (Georgan had three cats, and one night I overheard her whisper into a floppy ear, "I generally don't like dogs, but I love you."). I told them that, if Shirelle could be there on closing night, I'd insist on her getting the final bow. They agreed to that, but begged me to also bring her to an earlier show, which was being videotaped, so they could have her captured for posterity.

They were all terrific actors. But Wendy was phenomenal. The kitty scene became all I'd dreamt – with both her and David nearly getting their arms jerked out. Her Sylvia was bratty, overpowered, disarming, poignant, sexy, a great singer, a force every second. If this was fated to be my memorial statue to Shirelle, it was a worthy one.

*

Someone told me that in traditional Mexican beliefs, pets are our guardian angels, and take our diseases from us. If your dog gets sick, it was your disease. So after years of occasional stress-induced bingeing on cigarettes, I made a vow: Not

Another Puff, As Long As She Lives. For anything I smoked might go straight into her heart or liver.

*

Shirelle's behavior during rehearsals was perfect. She would play with the actors, and sniff around the old Morgan-Wixson (generally regarded as haunted), but once I tied her to her front-row chair, she'd stretch out and sleep – except when the prop toys were brought out.

A squeaky stuffed duck and a rubber ball with a bell in it occupied her attention from day one. She knew those were for a dog, and there was only one dog here. So the cast and crew had to always make sure they were out of reach whenever she got off her leash. And we encouraged her repeatedly, that if she were there on closing night, she'd have them all to herself forever.

*

I met with a veterinary oncologist. She confirmed that Sarcomas have no cure, though chemotherapy can slow them down. Chemo has far less negative effect on dogs than on people, partly because dogs don't go bald (it eliminates hair, not fur), but also apparently because they don't know they're being injected with poison.

But I was inclined against it. First, because *I* would know she was being poisoned, but secondly because she was so terrified to walk back into that hospital. Even if she didn't know what was happening, was it kind to extend a life where every couple of weeks she'd be traumatized by being left there threaded on IVs? Couldn't we just keep building her immune system with acupuncture to give her as much time as possible? But my vet disagreed, admitting that her insistence came from her not forgiving herself for stopping chemo on a beloved cat who'd died recently.

There was no right answer. My dad commented, "It's a shame animals can't write living wills."

I was driving with Shirelle, thinking about this, when she started panting frantically. As if we were back at Mile 26. I turned to her and asked, "Puppy, do you want me to do chemo?" No response. "Do you want me *not* to do chemo?" Nothing. I couldn't get any sense from her, so went back to driving, and muttered a thought out loud, "Maybe Mala could tell me something." And at that instant, Shirelle stopped panting. I looked at her eyes, "Do you want me to ask Mala?" She licked a couple of times.

Mala was a doctor who'd ridded me of a plethora of allergies a few years earlier, using a method called NAET, or Nambudripad Allergy Elimination Treatment, that mixed homeopathy, chiropractic, and acupuncture. Could it help her as well? And was she saying it might?

Maybe dogs can write living wills after all, as long as we can read them.

*

A few prize moments:

- Sylvia meeting the matron, and humping her repeatedly, wasn't working. Wendy was doing just what a dog would do, bouncing from the knees, and it simply wasn't funny. Then one night (I never knew how she came up with it), she ran up to matron Gregory, clamped her knees around his thighs, and began bouncing from her *ankles*, faster than I could imagine possible. Suddenly, it was innocent and filthy – she had become Shirelle!

- Spending a long night with Georgan and David, making up a history of their marriage (largely based on their own experiences), creating an eerily beautiful relationship.

- And a Woman-of-the-Rock moment, when we all took a break in the lobby, and walked back in, but stopped – struck by the force of seeing Shirelle posed proudly on the set, chest out, head erect, possessed of an eerie power, looking curiously at us, as if to say, "I didn't expect to see you here in my theater tonight!"

And it really did become her theater, and not just because of the appalling amount of fur shed into their carpeting. The theater staff, other shows' casts and crews, all simply fell in love with her. You could feel the healing power of it.

*

I saw August Wilson's new play, *Radio Golf.* There was a lovely line in it about how perfect days are the most sad, because you know they're bound to end.

I don't know how long she's got. But this perfect day, this years-long perfect day, is going to end sometime. Maybe very soon.

*

We had only one major technical problem. The theater was very deep, and they couldn't project a slide far enough for the image at the end of the show to be clear. Instead, a friend who worked at a print shop blew up a new picture I took of Shirelle to five feet square, and we fixed it behind a painting on the set. At the end of the show, the stage manager had the delicate job of lowering the painting slowly from backstage, while light faded up, to reveal, just ever so perfectly, the giant smiling head of... well, for these purposes, Sylvia.

*

Mala did a test on Shirelle, to see if chemo was a good idea, and said she didn't know why, but the answer was, "Don't do it." Maybe because Shirelle had too little time to live, maybe because she didn't need it. "But wait, why don't we look at what caused this?" She tested, and said, "There's a virus she caught in her water."

She started to teach me a way to strengthen Shirelle against the illness, when I bolted upright: *Did Shirelle do this?* My question had been about doing chemo or not. Did Shirelle send me here to find out about the water? Was she telling me one more part of how to save her life?

The first time working on the virus energy was extremely hard on both of us. She shed lots of hair, I absorbed lots of pain, and the energy coming out was exhausting. The same sort of energy that came out in the acupuncturist's office. And then...

That day her collar got too tight. She'd been expanding so much that it needed to be loosened two notches.

By the next day, outside of her long scar, she looked just like a month before.

My intellectual brain was saying, "Probably we have very little time left." But my gut felt she was healing. This was so difficult, annoying, wonderful.

*

Meanwhile, there was another element to the show. A weird one. I had never seen so many coincidences. Georgan had once worked with Wendy's mother. Wendy had known her understudy, Jennifer, since birth – babysat her, even took her on vacation once. Other strange ties kept showing, adding to my overwhelming feeling that this was something much more than a play. But just what all this serendipity meant – good mojo or terrible – no one could say. For example, our costume designer had directed me in a play a few years earlier, a romantic comedy about love after death, during which her husband passed away. In the end, the play helped her through it, which was a magic of its own, but I didn't want that experience. I wanted the impossible.

In my favorite of the coincidences, just before we opened, the theater had a short run of a children's production of *Peter Pan*. I showed up early for rehearsal one day, while they were building their sets, to go over costumes with our lead actress. I saw her empty car outside and knew she must be in the theater, so walked across the stage calling, "Wendy? Are you here?" And suddenly realized I was yelling those words in the Darling children's bedroom!

*

A month after Shirelle's operation, and the day before her birthday, I decided to take her on a trip to our favorite beach. But before we left, the car had problems, I misplaced my credit card, obstacle after obstacle in the way. "I can't believe this. I just want to be nice to my dog for her birthday, can't I do anything?!" But wait, was it a sign?

I asked Shirelle whether we should go or not, but any responses she gave seemed nebulous, not answers at all.

We finally left, avoiding bad drivers, the whole world just craziness. By the time we arrived, the sun was beginning to go down already. I took a roll of pictures as Shirelle ran around.

It grew so dark I couldn't see her. Scary, but then a bit of slight white in the black. I relaxed. The stars were beautiful and all felt enchanted.

We got in the car. I was exhausted and very hungry. As it was her birthday in a few hours, we stopped for burgers, for both of us.

We got home, and she seemed detached. Didn't even want a snack, so I had to shove her pills down her throat. I pulled her up onto the bed and knocked out to sleep.

Two hours later, I was awakened by an awful sound. She'd started gagging, big gags, like she was going to throw up. And then panting, rapid-fire. My heart froze. Not today. Not now. Not her birthday.

I took her outside, she walked around, squatted to poop, nothing came. Heaving and hacking, her tongue extending way down out of her mouth. Her belly growing bigger and bigger. A nightmare from Dante, but staring at me with frightened eyes begging that it stop.

I ran her to the hospital. The doctor took one look at her and rushed her back. He took x-rays to be sure, but he knew.

Because of the space from her spleen's removal, her stomach had flipped in her now-roomier abdominal cavity, and twisted like a balloon animal, cutting off everything from coming in or going out. He said he could turn it back over and attach it to the inner wall, that it would be a quick surgery, 30-45 minutes. But that it was dangerous, a 20 percent chance of death if there were complications. And because of the splenectomy and sarcoma, her life expectancy was poor. So I should probably just put her down.

Again. No. Do the surgery (so grateful for that pet insurance).

The bloat operation went smoothly, but during it, I was convinced a few times she'd died, because I felt those chills, deeper than ever. He said the anesthesia does that, makes them very cold. Again we were each other.

I saw her knocked-out body, gutted again. The doctor mentioned he found onions in her stomach. And I suddenly heard Shirelle's vet telling me, a very long couple of months ago, that dogs have trouble digesting onions, and if I give Shirelle a burger it shouldn't have any.

And what had I done that day? Had her body running and playing, flipping that stomach round, and then gave her a burger, with onions. For all practical purposes, I had murdered her.

I went home, my soul on dry ice. I couldn't sleep. And when I tried, my exhaling was frozen. Deep in pain, in guilt and self-loathing.

About a week before this, adding to the changes the acupuncturist had suggested, I'd gone to a small store of Chinese goods, and taken the owner's advice on some symbols and talismans to have in my home to continue improving the Feng Shui. The week had been difficult, many things hadn't moved forward with the show, all felt stifled. Now, with all this oppressive energy in the house, even beyond my own guilt and remorse, I looked at the little statues – could they be contributing? I put them in a bag, stuck them in the garage, and went to see Shirelle, barely daring to ask how she was.

And amazingly, out she came. Five hours after the operation – and a month after the splenectomy – she was lively and eager for a walk. And quite peeved when I had to leave her there for more care. Her recovery was phenomenal. The staff talked of nothing else, had never seen anything like it.

I came home to phone messages that we'd gotten a set builder and a lighting designer. And a repairman I'd been trying to reach all summer came by.

I took that bag of Chinese goods straight to Goodwill. Good riddance!

Then the *Sylvia* cast came to my house for a rehearsal. I didn't want to admit my sins, but I was safe – no one seemed to notice she wasn't there anyway. Good Lord, actors are narcissistic!

Eventually I brought it up. "I have to admit, I'm pretty shocked, but doesn't it seem someone's missing?" Breathlessly, they explained – every time my back had turned, they'd been exchanging fearful looks and questions, convinced she'd died and I was in deep denial.

What an idiot I can be!

So this must be what they call awareness. If the day before had gone smoothly, if the car hadn't acted up, and I hadn't lost my card, things might have been different. Maybe we would have gotten to the beach early enough to play longer, Shirelle's bloat would have happened a hundred miles away from home, and she would have died on the way to a vet.

Surely if I'd chosen chemotherapy, the poison in her system would have been too much for her to handle in the operation, and we'd have lost her.

And what if the bloat hadn't happened that night, at that hour? What if she'd made it through just fine, and then one day, when I was off working, she chased squirrels ferociously and caught and ate one, so it occurred when I wasn't home? She'd be gone.

Everything, from the NAET session to the trouble traveling, to the onions in the burger, had turned out as well as possible. Did she do this? Call it God, call it Coincidence, call it the Blue Fairy if you want, but it's hard to see it as accidental.

Then look at her astounding recovery – on her birthday no less – as though she knew she had had to go through this, but was now ready to embrace the future.

A few morals here. One is to respect the delicacy of someone who's had an operation, no matter how much energy she might have. Another is not to toy with things that have power: You wouldn't buy medicine from some stranger on the street, so why would you buy charms to change the Qi of your house from a little booth? And most important is not to lose hope, continue being grateful, because things might be for the best.

But what did it all mean? I didn't know. I only knew one thing.

And here it was: "I have Shirelle. The play will go up, she's doing great, and is coming home soon. And as a birthday present, she's beaten death yet again.

"How can I complain? I've got Shirelle, I've got Shirelle, I've got Shirelle!"

*

Opening nights always arrive too soon. And I didn't like being in the theater away from my girl (we couldn't have her in the audience, and she was uncomfortable being locked up backstage).

The program had a bio for her, as Technical Director, as well as my notes telling of her life, her badness, her magic, and what the play meant to me. Ending with…

And naturally, it's dedicated to all of them. The tumbling-mate, the stolen, the martyred rebel, the insecure saint, the neurotic beauty, and every other one out there, in homes, in pounds, on the streets – but most of all to her. The guardian angel who has ruled and tickled my heart, every moment, these eleven blessed years.

Heal. Stay.

*

Even with tech glitches, the show opened well. Gregory was as precise as ever, Georgan stressed and lovely, David giving just enough energy and power to make us fall in love with his soft heart. But Wendy, I don't have words. I wanted young Shirelle, and she gave it with both barrels. And with a loud, boisterous audience, the night was a joy throughout.

And yes, I did burst into tears when Shirelle's giant picture came up. She was healing incredibly, but all I'd held in all this time was right there at that moment. Especially when, as at every performance, they would say Sylvia stayed with them eleven years before dying. That was exactly Shirelle's age at the time.

*

The box-office far surpassed expectations, word of mouth was great, *Sylvia* was a hit. The cast stayed strong, the understudies came through beautifully, and at each performance, over a hundred people fell in love with Sylvia. With the most common comment: "I forgot I was watching a person. I totally accepted that she was a dog."

I'd help clean up every night, celebrate over a drink with the cast, and then speed home, but hesitate to open my front door, in fear the inevitable had happened.

But then, the day of closing... it hadn't. She was still there. Doing great. I sat holding her that morning, and wondered how. Was it the acupuncture? The chiropractic adjustments? The NAET? Herbs, the Feng Shui of the house, the bell on her neck? Yes, I thought. But more as well.

Around this time, an idea that had been around for just a few thousand years was gaining newfound popularity – the "secret" of manifestation. The concept that if one concentrates enough on what they wish for, that wish can become actualized (and similarly, if one's thoughts are routinely negative, that pessimism will serve as a self-fulfilling prophecy). Shirelle's health seemed related to this, but not in the sense that she healed because I'd meditated on her healing. Rather it was because I had done *everything* to make it happen.

There's an energy – I'd seen it in creative pursuits before – where the act of going overboard, doing every single thing possible for something, creates a higher energy than the sum of its parts. Was Shirelle alive today, I wondered, not because of any one of the healing things I'd done for her, but because of all of them? The old saying that God helps those who help themselves, but with the added words, "but only completely, not casually."

And yet, was even that enough? She'd been given a death sentence, and she was her full energetic self. Something else, something... and an epiphany came to me. So funny, and so clearly right. That night, before the show, I told the cast how much each of them meant to me. And then I told them about what I'd grasped.

It was from that cute *Peter Pan* incident. You see a good production of *Peter Pan* or a bad one, there's one moment that'll work. You know it: It's when Tinkerbell, Peter's steady companion, best friend, has drunk the poison, and her light starts to flicker. And Peter realizes what's happened and looks out to the audience and says that her weakness is because we have grown too cynical. And that the only thing that can cure her is if we clap our hands, to prove that we still believe in fairies.

And everyone starts to cry and to clap, and her light gets stronger and they clap harder, and the light gets full, and all's well and off to vengeance on Captain Hook.

And that's exactly what our show did. My Tinkerbell was full of poison. I and so many magicians did all we could. But something even bigger happened: These actors, for two hours, made that audience *believe* that they were watching *A Dog*.

And then, in the most brilliant moment of the play, they believe so much that, when Greg and Kate say they had to put Sylvia down, the audience always cries, and the picture shows up.

And the audience's minds snap back, in an "Oh, that's right!" moment, mixing with laughter at the silly face and tears at the sweetness of it. And the forgiveness and understanding and redemption and love of Greg and Kate's marriage, and the power and goofiness of the dog, glow in their bodies. Because they believe. And they see the soft light. And they clap. And it's Shirelle. And the light gets stronger. And all that love, all the love that had been earned by my work and many others', and the cast's brilliance, and most of all Gurney's words and vision – all the love that audience feels feeds straight into that picture.

And so, Shirelle lives. She beat the poison. Because they believed.

Of course, with that, I got everyone in the cast weeping before the performance even began. But it was our best audience ever, so they cheered right up.

The show ended, the applause was huge, the cast came out and bowed, and I was all ready to walk up on stage after Shirelle's curtain call… but there was no Shirelle. I ran back in terror, found the bored confused dog still locked up in a dressing room, and pulled her onto the stage yelling out, just like Gene Kelly, "Wait! This is what the show was all about, this is the real star!" And the audience turned and applauded her, and she leapt off the stage into their adulation.

Turns out in all the confusion, no one had planned who would bring her out! Like everything else about the show, and her, it was imperfect and glorious.

And after all was cleared up and shut down, Wendy threw a party. I brought Shirelle, who honored the holy experience by chasing her cat down the street.

*

That Christmas, I pose Shirelle in front of the 5x5 *Sylvia* poster for a card. A squirrel makes a noise above her, and she looks up, intense.

By this time she'd reduced her acupuncture sessions to every couple of months, instead of three times a week. The fur on her abdomen had grown back, and she looked perfect.

No one who received the card knew she was looking at a squirrel. They saw what I saw in it, a proud and powerful beast who had faced down certain death.

*

And then, on the morning of July 26, 2006, I was comfortably sleeping, the sun was just starting to rise, and Shirelle jumped onto the bed and woke me.

YES!!! YES!!! Look what happened! Look what we did!

It had been a year. Her bark had gone from deafening to raspy, but otherwise she seemed as healthy as when she still had her spleen.

I took her to the acupuncturist, who gave her her usual treatment.

Then I talked about her in the substance abuse groups I was running, and the members seemed to understand my argument about my not smoking: Maybe it's silly, maybe it has nothing to do with her health, but I'm not taking the chance. So why do you guys take these chances?

And I did what I'd promised myself I'd do. Made a ton of phone calls. Medical practitioners, neighbors, friends who'd prayed, others who'd dog-sat. But most importantly I called every cast and crew member of that show to thank them for the magic. Some people were thrilled, while others were mystified at my weirdness.

The next day, I took her back to the surgeon to get some tests. It took the pup about 90 seconds. First she was running around the reception area, sniffing, jumping up on counters, being silly. And then it sparked: "Oh! That's where I am!" and she lunged at the big glass door to get out. Trembling like crazy.

The surgeon's assistant brought him the file in his office. He looked at it and sighed. "Oh, yes. I remember this case. A very sweet dog. And the owner was so loving, so sad. But you've brought me the wrong file. Because this dog's dead."

"Oh?" she queried. "Then what's this?" She opened the door, and the Knucklehead galloped in and splashed onto him.

I stood in a waiting room, cold and frightened. Eventually, he walked out to me, and told me about her entrance. He then paused, to confess. "I am in shock. I don't know what to say to you. I have never, in my entire career, seen someone beat this. I need to tell you, we sort of lied to you, we do it to everyone. We just want your last days together to be happier. Shirelle didn't have two months. In the shape she was in, she didn't have two weeks.

"Nobody lives through this. And I have to tell you, I just did an abdominal ultrasound, I looked at the lung and liver and heart, and she is perfectly clean."

I lost my balance, almost fell over. Not fainting, just my legs giving out.

"She's free," he continued. "There's no other word for this but Miracle."

So I told him about the play. As a traditional Western-medicine surgeon, he's of course trained not to accept such nonsense. But he just looked up at me with bewildered eyes and said, "That's as good an explanation as any."

It felt so good. But I realized I hadn't thanked the one person who was arguably most important. It was time to write A.R. Gurney. I'd recently learned that some friends of mine actually knew him, and got his email address from them.

I wrote him the story, and asked if he could send me his address, so I could mail him the triumphant Christmas card. He wrote back a nice, short, appreciative note, but no address. I imagine my enthusiasm terrified him.

She had done the impossible. She was perfectly clean. She was strong. She had beaten it. I knew she was still prone to cancers. I wasn't saying she was immortal.

But I did walk out of that hospital muttering "Death Be Not Proud!"

While at my side walked "no other word but…"
Miracle.

Chapter Sixteen:
Fame

When I was young, the Zeitgeist was owned by certain performers or shows for a year or more. In seventh grade, Elton John ruled. My last years in high school, *Saturday Night Live* and its cast virtually controlled our minds.

Twenty years later, though, the public focus seemed to change by the month, if not the week. And on the night of May 14, 2006, the collective mindset of the United States was owned by *Grey's Anatomy*.

I didn't watch much television anymore. But I would watch things that friends performed on or wrote. And my buddy Mark (whose pregnant wife Darcy's sweater Shirelle had ripped as a puppy) was now writing for *Grey's*. So I was a regular viewer.

Grey's Anatomy is an eccentric soap opera about the lives of interns at a large Seattle hospital. The primary focus at this time was on the fluctuating relationship between the beautiful but deeply attachment-disordered Dr. Meredith Grey and the handsome, brilliant, but conflicted Dr. Derek Shepherd.

At this point in the saga, Derek and Meredith have become co-owners of a dog, Doc, while she's started dating his handsome and kind veterinarian Dr. Finn Dandridge. Doc seems to be doing badly, and something big is bound to happen, as the season is about to end.

I got my aching body into a hot bath, turned on the television, and – "Hey, tonight's episode was written by Mark!"

And while all sorts of turgid events were transpiring (one intern stealing a heart from another operation to give to her dying boyfriend), Finn explained that Doc had a particularly aggressive form of cancer, a Sarcoma.

I should mention here that, a couple of months earlier, I'd had dinner with Mark and Darcy, and told them the story of the Miracle, "and this would be so good on the show! It would be a great problem for the doctors, as an incurable disease disappears by non-medical means!" Mark always has played his cards close to his vest, but agreed it was a great tale. So, could this be…?

I yelled to Shirelle to come in and watch with me, but, afraid I was going to bathe her, she stayed away. I sat transfixed through the hour, till Meredith finally approached Finn about the prognosis, and he explained that the dog didn't have long to live…

Forget the stolen heart! I rushed, dripping, to my computer. "Mark! I don't want to hear anything about the next episode, so I'm not phoning to tell you this show was great. But, whether it was a conscious choice of yours or not, Sarcoma is what Shirelle had, and we're very honored over here!"

In the morning he wrote me back, "Glad you like it. And absolutely, this was for my friend Shirelle!"

I was beside myself. Wrote emails to everyone I could think of, saying, "You have to watch! You'll see how Shirelle got saved!"

And when the next episode aired, with my Miracle cradled in my arms, I sat in front of my TV to soak it up...

Whoops.

Seems Mark only got to use the one word, and not the story. The Sarcoma had spread, and the vet euthanized Doc. So I called their home, "Hey Darcy, your #@&%! husband killed my dog on national television!"

I was a bit embarrassed about my effusive emails, but figured that was the end of the story.

Oh no. This is the thing about the Zeitgeist.

Ever since that day, Shirelle will come into a conversation I'll have with a new acquaintance, and they'll react as to any other dog. And then I'll mention *Grey's*. And their countenance changes – suddenly I'm an intimate friend of theirs, because they had wept, they had cared so much, for the dog with the Sarcoma.

I had tried, in so many ways, to honor Shirelle with fame. The feature film, the commercial, hundreds of Christmas cards sent around the world, *Sylvia*, and none had really accomplished it.

But this did. She became "the *Grey's Anatomy* dog." Even if the only thing she had in common with the TV character was a disease.

I suggested to Mark that Meredith might hear about something like Shirelle's Miracle, which would make her furious with Finn for unnecessarily killing her dog and she could leave him, since the entire world wanted her to get back with Derek anyway. But no, she left him for being too nice a guy. Happens to us every time.

A couple of years later, Meredith had a near-death experience, where in her mind she saw Doc again. The day after it aired, Mark called. "Did you see last night's show?"

"Yeah."

"Well? You're welcome!"

"Hey, this doesn't change anything! That dog's still dead!"

"Okay, I guess you're right."

But how much extra affection that poor dead mutt got Shirelle! I picked her, I chose her, but now everybody loved her.

151

Part Five:

Partnership

Chapter Seventeen:
Age

What was I to her, and she to me? Was she Johnson to my Boswell, me recording her wisdom for prosperity? Was I Cathy to her Heathcliff, tied to society such that I couldn't join in her earthy truth? Annie Sullivan to her Helen Keller, working tirelessly with a difficult child to aid her in communication of brilliance? Was I simply a caretaker, a codependent fan happy to serve?

Or were we what I liked to think – equals in mutual estimation, with different strengths? In *Rio Bravo*, when John Wayne is asked why he keeps taking care of pathetic drunk Dean Martin, he responds that Martin's been doing "a pretty good job o' takin' care a' me!"

I kept her safe, fed, healthy, and sheltered, while she gave me security, laughter, warmth, and soul. I taught her to sit and shake hands and that many people don't like being jumped on, while she taught me to stop and smell the fire hydrants.

I helped her stay alive, while she showed me how to live. And that had worked for a decade.

But now, after these horrors and raptures, we were changed. Dogs always seem to fear, when their people leave them, that they will never come back. Well, once I learned of the cancer, every time I left her, I was equally worried that she wouldn't be there when I returned. Often, I would walk in and find her not at the door. And with terror, I'd rush back to find her lovingly greet me, both of us understanding that she'd have to stretch her aging muscles a minute more before she'd be up to jumping off the bed.

So we finally had progressed to the same plane, where every hello, which had previously been joy, was now a mutual "Thank Heaven you're here!" Life wasn't just near each other anymore, it was about each other.

Before this, she was the best dog I'd ever had. But now, we were partners.

*

In *Tuesdays With Morrie*, Morrie says everyone's going to die, but we don't believe it, and that's why we live as though we're not going to.

My ethos had always been "You'd better accomplish this before you die." But that's different from living as though it's my last day on earth. It was all about my bitterness at my lack of accomplishment.

But now, I lived constantly expecting Shirelle's death.

I'd thought about it often before – how I'd deal with it. But now I had some idea of what it would put me through. So my mind did all it could to brace me. Which took some of the easy joy out of having her company, of course.

Meanwhile Shirelle lived with no apparent awareness of death, but each moment, as always, lived to the fullest. The airwaves had been filled with Tim McGraw's uplifting "Live Like You're Dying," but that would have made no sense to Shirelle. Live *like?* Naah, that's just for humans. For her, living wasn't *like* anything. It was everything.

*

This funny thing happened to me all the time. I'd look over at the mutt on the floor, and feel nothing for it, and then suddenly I'd fall in love again. And have this realization – I really do like my dog; and isn't that interesting, because it's just a dog.

Others saw her as all I cared about. No. No more than I was all she cared about. We only gave each other priority in decisions. The emotion came and went.

It's just that when it came, it was so overwhelming!

*

One of my first therapy placements was close to a friend's house; conveniently he'd just bought a Golden Retriever puppy. So, that day every week, I left Shirelle there. It was beautiful karmic revenge – he was as hyperactive and destructive as she had once been, while she was now the curmudgeon who didn't care for his rough play. She'd want to sniff and lay out, while he wanted to tumble.

One particularly fine day, I put her in the yard and patted him while she sniffed about. When she squatted to pee, he broke away and broadsided her onto the ground.

It was then that I learned that an old long-jawed dog can fully bite a young Golden's butt and cause searing pain, but with no injury.

*

At times she would walk up to me and bow her head down slightly and just press her forehead into me – my leg, my arm, my chest. To absorb some strength, asking for quiet understanding love.

An act of deep trust, and overwhelming humble beauty.

*

I'm hiking with her in a brushy area, and I see rabbits. I try to show them to her, but she's more interested in some trashcans. Rabbits are better, but she knows trashcans.

I enjoy new experiences if they're fun, but I too seek more the thrill of deepening learning about the familiar. I never tire of looking at Shirelle. There's always something new there. I don't tire of certain old movies, or music I've heard before. I'm fascinated by my family's history.

So when choosing a career, friends, a mate, it's good to ask if this is something you'll want to learn more about forever.

*

We developed yet another shorthand. I'd see her gazing at me, and, knowing I had no words to translate what was in her eyes, or speak what they brought out in me, I would just say, from the bottom of my heart, "And I you."

Chapter Eighteen:
Passion

She admitted that she'd acted the way she had in our relationship because she wanted to maintain control. And that I should accept that and try yet again with her. But no one wants to be loved by someone maintaining control.

It feels like a dictatorship of the soul. To feel loved, I want to be able to get excited by it, lose myself in the moment. How can I if someone else is always grabbing control?

And how often do I do the same? A friend said, "If you want to be loved, you have to put out the part of you that might be hated." Isn't holding that back a way of staying in control?

Besides, taking it further, isn't letting someone else be in control a passive way of keeping control? Keeping the relationship from going anywhere, or growing?

Is it possible to honor self-control in another's life outside of the romance, but to undo it when in the romance?

Doesn't that define romance?

As Shirelle does what she is told, and stays in the yard even when the gate's open, but dives on people she loves, and begs to play fetch or tug-of-war beyond all control.

She knows love, and how to be loved.

*

How would it feel to be passionate about everything? To, instead of sighing, "I haven't accomplished anything today," exult, "There's so much I want to do!"

In *Limelight*, Charlie Chaplin argues that life isn't a meaning but a desire. But Shirelle would disagree slightly; she'd say the meaning of life is Passion.

Look at this world. There is no intrinsic universally-accepted value to anything. People sacrifice their environment, communities, children, their own lives – even risk, in their beliefs, their immortal souls – for their passions. And it's that sacrifice, the value they put on their passions, that gives their lives meaning.

No wonder I was always depressed when my plays closed. What I had been passionate about was lost. And if life without Passion is life without meaning, then the meaning of my life at that time was suddenly gone. The joke is that, when we've lost Passion, we often try to think of passions, or distractions, to keep us from feeling depressed, while depression is usually the clearest map we have to finding our next real passion. Besides, searching that way for a passion is inevitably futile – trying to use your brain to tell your heart what to feel.

In *Zen and the Art of Motorcycle Maintenance*, Robert Pirsig defines Quality as the other thing besides mind and body, and states that one can see Quality in a great work of art or a finely tuned engine.

But Quality is so detached a concept. It's a result; what causes Quality?

I say it's Passion. When he talks about the way a good craftsman or an artist loses himself in his work, that's Passion. It's Passion that takes over, so much so that he might lose awareness and sensation; the creation becomes an outside-of-self experience, a loss of ego.

So when we see a great work of art, and say, "Wow, I don't even know how that was done," we're right. We can't know, because it was created by Passion.

Just in case I miss the point of all this, who's there? Running around, chasing, barking? Somebody who finds Passion in her reactions to everything.

(And it's interesting to then note that the Crucifixion is referred to as the Passion, as it's the central element of a revelation of godliness and meaning.)

*

Every night, I'd give her a preventative NAET rubdown, saying with no fear of being wrong, "Nobody ever loved anything more than I love my Knucklehead."

*

It's amazing how distant people are from even those nearby these days. But that still doesn't explain the fact that I had lived on this street for years before ever bumping into a woman who lived three doors down, with whom I'd worked closely before moving there. Marie and her husband Eric became like family the second we re-connected. This included Marie asking me to lift their ailing dog into a car to go to a vet, which turned out to be her last ride.

The hole in their lives caused by Molly's loss was searing, and only had one cure. Paging Doctor Poophead. She was everything they needed.

And like dream grandparents, they adopted Shirelle and showered her with love that, heretofore, only I had given. I stopped hiring dog-sitters; when I left town, they took her, refusing thanks, just pouring out gratitude for having her in their home. And she loved them like nothing I'd ever seen. Walks down the block now weren't just struggles to keep her from chasing squirrels or other dogs; I also had to keep her from lunging through their front door.

And now here we were, at their house, celebrating Thanksgiving, but also Shirelle's and my twelfth anniversary. Meaning we'd beaten the We-kept-her-eleven-years-and-then-had-to-put-her-down *Sylvia* threat.

I paused, unnoticed, by the kitchen, while Eric was carving the turkey.

As she sat attentively by his feet. And he put one piece on the platter to serve to the people, and gave one to her. One to us, one to her, one to us, one to her… How beautiful. He was so happy, she was so happy, I was so happy.

Thanks all around.

Chapter Nineteen:
Validation

I loved my psychotherapy work that year, except that I needed to earn a living, and wasn't doing so. I hadn't changed careers for charity. I would have a great day at the nonprofit clinic I worked at, and then beat myself up all the way home for living in debt. I began searching for an internship that I could fully live on. A search that would take over six demeaning months.

It was like trying to sell the feature all over again. Every unreturned phone call, every "we're sorry but it doesn't seem a good fit;" even "We'd hire you in a second, but our insurance won't let us because of those two speeding tickets" would send me tornadoing, "Nobody, *nobody* needs this long to find a job they're more than qualified for! I'm doing ten times as much as anyone else I know, to accomplish the simplest things. I'm so sick of this #$%&@!!"

But I'd always pull back on seeing Shirelle, afraid to put this bad feeling into her. Whatever else happened, she was there, and I had oceans of reason for gratitude.

*

So round, so powerful. Too large for the thin legs, like a puppy who never grew up. When she stands, they stick out to the side, but when she lies down they extend straight from her.

Miraculous, so sensitive with those muscles, tendons, and nerves so close to the surface on top. The toenails that crack up to expose the meat of her fragile digits if she should step wrong.

And the pads – all we ask of our shoes and more, thick, protective, the color of earth because they are one with it. Yet, as she is both wild and domestic, they divide, with the vulnerable softness of short white fur pressing out between them like grass through old asphalt.

As I hold her feet, press, massage the tops, investigate, she tightens. This most armored part of her, that takes the impact punch every time she runs, jumps, pounces, climbs, stops, turns, slips, or pulls back, is also her most delicate. And loving the massaging, but fearful of the wrong pull (as when I trim her nails), she both tenses and tries to relax, like a human.

*

I'd looked to others for validation my whole life. And sometimes they had filled that need, but not for long. Even if they stuck around, the validation disappeared.

In the midst of this demeaning job search, I realized that what I'd really sought over decades was just to be validated from the outside. Please say I'm good, say I'm cool, I'm worthy, wantable, worth buying, acceptable.

And here was the joke: Eventually, *every one of those requests had been met.*

Maybe not as fully as I'd like, or by the person I'd want to do it. But I'd been wanted, I'd been considered very good, I'd sold lots of tickets.

So the truth was that no one on the outside was going to validate me. Even if someone wanted to, and stuck around, they simply *couldn't.* No one can. Ever.

God knows, no one could have had more worth in my eyes than Shirelle, or loved me more, and she couldn't validate me. So why think someone else could?

So the answer was: Stop looking for it.

This wasn't some New Age platitude about validating oneself. That's a fine goal, but I was being harsher. I was saying "Give up! It's not going to happen. Accept that deep down you feel not good enough. Move on!"

Later on the day I had that thought, I got a call from a large clinic, offering me a terrific job, and said yes. Months of humiliation came to a happy, and very quiet, end (except for all the phone calls I made singing The Miracles' "I Got a Job!").

Ironically though, this happiness also created a loss of motivation.

For the first time, I was engaged in my life without frantic seeking. So there was no thrill. I went out with woman after woman, wondering what she could offer me that would replace the excitement of my former neurotic need. The answer was nothing, so we would have a nice dinner and it wouldn't go anywhere else. I'd just hurt her if it did.

Meanwhile, there she was. Shirelle. Amazing Shirelle. Validation's so overrated!

*

While the large mental health center answered my financial concerns, I also took a part-time job at a small clinic where I could see a few clients I'd brought along with me. And I had an idea. I'd never tried to register Shirelle as a therapy dog, but that was only necessary for advertising. If the clients at this clinic were willing, could I bring her in with me? The big center's insurance wouldn't allow it, but maybe here? The supervisor agreed, and so did every one of my clients.

I simply saw this as a delightful chance to have more time together. But it also marked a new chapter for her, yet another cliff of triumph for her to scale.

She loved, after all these years, being allowed to accompany me to work, and proved a surprisingly calm co-therapist. She would greet everyone with sniffs and kisses, and then retire to a corner of the room to sleep for the hour. Immediately, our clients relaxed, felt more welcome, spoke more openly, and, when they needed to divert their attention from difficult topics, had a warm and friendly subject on which to focus.

But over time, she took on her role more fully.

- One client was stuck in self-flagellating rumination, when, across the room, Shirelle let out a deep groan and sigh. The client burst into laughter, suddenly exposed to the ridiculousness of his negativity.

- Later, sensing a desire for play, Shirelle got a young British girl, who had shown no desire to engage in therapy after enduring a difficult divorce, to embrace sessions passionately, as chances to be with this new best friend.

- And, on a few occasions, when a client would sit in a cut-off pain, unable to explode in needed fury or tears, Shirelle would purposefully get up, walk across the room, and lay her head in their lap. The effect: overwhelming.

Obviously, such a gesture lies well outside a therapist's ethical boundaries. But besides that, Shirelle's acts were so pure that clients had to read her acceptance and love as truth, and find themselves worthy – while anything a shrink says can be read as "therapeutic." Ironically, she was giving them what I couldn't accept from her – irrefutable validation.

Twice, though, her prescience had deeper genius to it.

- In one instance, a middle-aged client brought her father to a session, and poured out a lifetime of pain and resentment at his decades of abandonment. The man, frightened by her intense feelings, withdrew into a stilted detached speech of defensiveness, devastating her, though he couldn't even see it. After a minute or two of this, with no visible provocation, Shirelle stood up, walked to the nervous man, angrily barked at him, "ROWL ROWL ROWL!!!" for ten seconds, stopped, went back to her corner, and curled up for more napping, leaving us all silent in shock. After a moment, I tried to put him at ease, saying she must have heard something in another room. But later on the phone, my client brought it up. "I don't think Shirelle heard any noise." "Yeah," I grinned, as we furtively washed away the pain of the session, "Neither do I."

- The other involved a client whom I'd met when she was court-mandated for drug abuse treatment after suffering addiction for decades. After a year of work, she managed to reach sobriety from everything but cigarettes. But, just when her life seemed to offer freedom at last, her Hepatitis-C-infected liver began raising the ammonia level in her blood, causing her to black out for days at a time. I didn't see her for a few weeks, but when her health improved, her mother brought her in for a session.

Midway through our talk, she began to fade. But she didn't close her eyes. Rather she went into a strong stare, burning into me, her back erect, her jaw clenched, as if she were furious. But it was clear that she was trying to communicate something. This went on for about ten minutes, till Shirelle rose, walked over, and stood next to her, staring at me equally intently.

Without her glare moving at all from me, or her jaw or posture relaxing, my client's arm reached over and began stroking Shirelle's head and back. They continued – the client petting, Shirelle standing there, both laser-focused into my eyes – while her mother and I watched in amazement.

But what else was new? I went to sleep every night amazed by her.

*

I looked over the pictures I'd taken of her that year, to pick out a holiday card. The best of them came from the ugliest of landscapes, a rock field out behind a gas station, and captured a glowing being who had not just beaten death, but changed through it. Lost in the image, I wrote down the words I heard it speak:

Love Thoughtlessly.
Relish the day.
If you're not in awe,
You're just not paying attention.

Chapter Twenty:
Cheating with Momentum

I was trying a dance step, and could do it right as long as I did it quickly, but my form was off if I slowed down. Ivy said I was "Cheating with Momentum," making the steps work by speed, instead of correct technique.

Maybe that was the only way I was able to live without being overtaken by constant fear of losing Shirelle. I think once we reach a certain level of experience, we Cheat With Momentum a lot in life.

*

On December fourth, I got a call from a friend that her sister had died. That night, another friend emailed me that her husband's father had passed on, and her son's best friend had committed suicide. The next morning, I heard that another friend's son had succumbed to an illness. Then my brother called me, saying his wife's aunt died yesterday and her mother was expected to as well later in the week. Six deaths in twelve hours. A day later, a good friend to Shirelle and me passed away as well.

Over the next year, this was the way things went. For much of it, at the very least, three deaths a week would come into my life. Most of them, like those first few, were people I didn't know, but close to people I cared for. Others were much nearer.

*

I found a rat in my house, amazingly gutsy. I'd see him running through the kitchen and living room. I tried to catch him in a lifesaving trap, but he ate the peanut butter off with no problem. So finally I put out a kill-trap and got him.

I had killed rats before, but I felt bad about this one, and buried him. There was something sweet about his spirit I liked.

Then I had a dream: There was a crash in my bedroom. I ran to it, where a nasty rat was running around on a drum set and had fallen onto the cymbals. I called Shirelle in, and we chased it out of the bedroom, through the living room, and into the kitchen. I tried to scare it out with a lot of noise, and it ran up the back of my refrigerator, and jumped off, right onto my face. I grabbed him off, but he got out of my hand and onto the floor. Shirelle grabbed him, and shook him and broke his neck, and I woke up.

*

I'm not sure how her leash got lost, but I buy a new one, the bottom half of it chain, the top half leather. Looks really cool. We're walking with a client in a park, talking about his fears, when she pulls away to chase a squirrel. We watch her run, so fast, so intent, when she suddenly trips and her chest slams into the ground. I look to see what's wrong, but she's running again.

It's the leash, bad engineering. Stupid thing catches under her paws automatically.

*

I'd lie in bed at night, petting her, and rest my hand on her chest. And feeling the continuing miracle of its beat, I'd swoon, saying, "This heart is the single greatest thing in the world. The ten best things in the world are all Shirelle."

*

Another dream: I'm on vacation. We're fishing, catch some very easily. Two feet long or so. Orange/flesh colored, with heads like seals. Once they're on the boat, they don't fight; you just have to break their necks by twisting their heads. We catch two. And the third one has such a sad sweet face, so willing to be sent to the next world, and I say, "We have to stop; this is too many." And I break its neck easily, quick snap.

I woke up, and realized the face, the eyes, were Shirelle's.

*

I went out with a friend for New Year's Eve, but the party was dull, and we both agreed to go to our homes before midnight.

Shirelle and I sat listening to an old-music radio show wish happiness, health, and prosperity, and count down the seconds. I wished her especially the health, as Guy Lombardo played "Auld Lang Syne."

Then a DJ came on and wished us all a happy and safe 2007, "It's gotta be better than 2006!" And played Bob Dylan's "I Shall Be Released." How happy that sounded.

Chapter Twenty-One:
The Wind

For St. Patrick's Day, we were invited to a party. A Marine friend from my old acting classes had been serving in Bosnia, and was back to his wife and son. His dog had been a playmate of Shirelle's a decade before, and I gladly brought her along, forgetting that that dog had passed away, and they'd replaced her with a puppy.

As we walked up to the house, the now full-grown new dog barked furiously at Shirelle, lunging at the fence. A girl in the yard worried about it, and I said, "Oh, just close the side gate, it'll be fine; she'll be shut up here in front, and we'll go in the back," where the party was. So we did, not thinking about the fact that this dog could run into the house, and out the back door.

It was almost supernatural. She sped out, around the crowd, knowing exactly where she was going, shot behind me and lunged at Shirelle. For the first time since she'd been a puppy, Shirelle got blindsided, hitting the ground and yelping. I reached in and pulled the attacker straight up into the air, not even thinking about any danger. But she went completely docile, didn't even struggle against me.

Shirelle was okay, but scared. The owners ran over in shock. This had *never* happened before; this was a friendly dog. They scoldingly rushed her into the house.

The rest of the night was a Shirelle love-fest. Everyone was all over her, crazy about her. Especially when we found a bit of blood on her face, where she'd been bitten below her left eye. A pretty woman with exactly Shirelle's hair color; a guy saying, "Man, if it was me, I'd shoot that dog." All seemed settled.

But later, when we went to bed, she was deeply shaken. We both slept fitfully through the night. I could tell I was absorbing a lot; at times I'd even see the attack, from her point of view, and feel that fear.

The next morning, the cut had swollen. As much as I knew she'd hate it, I took her to the vet. They shaved the wound, which now looked like she had a black eye.

And a strange wind came. For the next few days, strangers would walk up to us, saying things about a dog they used to have, or their sick dog. I gave them friendly advice about acupuncture and all, but... why were they drawn to me? What was going on?

There was something about that dog at the party. Like out of an old myth. Like a fierce energy that came out from the world to grab Shirelle and roar, "You're not a winner anymore, you're an old dog now."

*

The next night, Shirelle whined when I picked her up. I was hurting her. I didn't know how.

In the morning she was weak, as though something had happened to one of her legs. I was about to leave, and she wouldn't even stand up. I lifted her softly by her front, just to say, "What's with you?" And her back legs swung out. "Girl, what is this?" And she rolled over and emptied her bladder.

I rushed her back to the hospital. Her temperature was low and her gums were pale. They did some X-rays, and dropped the bomb:

"Her liver has tumors, and the reason for the cold and pale is that she's anemic, because one of them is leaking badly."

The Hemangiosarcoma had returned. It was finally doing what it had wanted to do for nearly two years.

So that's what that eerie dog attack was about.

*

From the last time, I knew what to do, and started making calls from the hospital.

A schoolteacher got her students sending good thoughts in a moment of silence. A girlfriend who'd broken up with me a year before started crying, "I haven't had enough time with your best friend." Neither had I. A yoga teacher had his class send energy to her every time they went into the Downward-Facing Dog position. Others were predictably cool. "Don't keep her alive for longer than is fair, don't keep her in pain." "It's been a good run, this is about her life expectancy anyway." And even, "Man, I even hate it when my plants die." None were being mean, or, in their minds, negative. They were all saying the same loving thing: "I share your loss." But these same people had been trying to share my loss two years earlier! Paraphrasing Monty Python, she was Not Dead Yet!

The vets did a transfusion of red blood cells, so she could get by this time. And that night, Wendy spent over an hour lying on the hospital floor with her, bringing *Sylvia* magic back in.

I was facing what I'd feared. A terror of life without her. People were saying, "You've got to be grateful for what you've had," but I already was. People said no dog was ever more loved, and that was true. But no dog ever had more reason to be.

I drove home alone late, and… more than 100 emails, phone calls, prayers, people posting her picture on their walls.

"Remember, George Bailey, no dog is a failure who has friends."

*

The issue was Packed Cell Volume, or PCV. The level of concentration of coagulating blood cells. If too low, she wasn't safe to leave the hospital.

I called at 4:30 a.m. The vet was blunt but kind. She could come home, but, "It's time for hospice care. That means burgers and ice cream and walks on the beach." If things went as she expected, this would probably be Shirelle's last trip home from the vet's. But if there were another miracle, then I might have to take her another time. Because she got bitten or broke her toe again or…

She was very out of it that whole day. Spent it with Eric, not wanting to eat or drink, or move around much, just slowly following him whenever he'd leave the room. In the morning, when I'd left her there, she'd given me a devastating look. I wondered if it meant, "You're never going to see me again." Or just, even though she was at her favorite house, "I need you with me. I can't deal with being abandoned right now."

That night the acupuncturist treated her and said he thought he could stop the bleeding. The next morning she was still weak, but propped up on the bed, looking out the window, eager to have a treat. Friends took shifts while I was at work. By that night, it seemed like the universe had turned slightly, and was on Shirelle's side now. It was 2005 all over again.

Barely able to walk, she followed whoever was watching her everywhere.

At our lowest, we cling. We don't want to be alone at all. We love even more. As when we're puppies, attachment is everything.

180

Something to think about as we build more homes for the aged. Are we making them sterile or warm? In *Soylent Green*, the dying are shown images of a healthy earth. Should they be of our families instead?

I tried to bring back her puppy energy by playing her Tom Petty's "Yer So Bad," along with "I Won't Back Down," over and over, to encourage her. And Kay Kyser, because she'd always liked that. Songs like "Who Wouldn't Love You?"

*

We were sleeping hard. Then she bolted up panicked. Panting. I was so exhausted that I was still half-dreaming. The dream was about work. My good clients' folders were in good shape, while the bad clients' covers were dilapidated, torn, falling apart. And I knew I needed to focus on the good client, who was next to me.

It wasn't until late the next day that I remembered that dream, and realized what it said. Shirelle had been next to me. She was the good client. She was what mattered.

*

I saw two scenarios. Worst case was that she had a very limited time in front of her. The other was that she had much more. If scenario one was right, then I wanted to give her all the love and attention and spoiling I could, as the vet had said. If two was right, the key, as I learned before, was… to give her all the love and attention and spoiling I could.

In other words, I was freed. Outside of taking her to healers (whom I wouldn't have bothered with if I didn't think she had a chance), I just did whatever felt right.

*

When was it? When did it happen? I liked the dog at first. But I remember driving home from the pound, looking at her in the back seat, wondering, "Is this really the dog I want?" And so many other moments when she was such a pain.

I know I fell in love with her first bark. But when did it go higher? When did I say, "This is the best thing that ever happened to me?" Maybe when she laid her head on my heart? And the mystery began?

These things need to be appreciated. These things need to be noted. A beautiful old song kept running through my head: "A heart that's true, there are such things…"

*

In the midst of this dizziness, a child therapist I'd pursued for two years called, wanting to hire me. My dream job. If only Shirelle could get better, I'd be able to take her with me to work all the time, and my hours would be halved. It could be the best year of our lives.

*

By two weeks later, I felt like the big April Fool's joke had been on me. She wasn't quite back to where she'd been before, but she was close, and still improving.

I came home and hugged her. I'd been so delicate with her these last weeks, but she was doing great, so I lifted her up slightly, like we'd always done.

Her back legs slid out from under her and she fell hard onto the floor. And just lay there for a second, breathing, blinking, like a shot deer.

Oh, God, the remorse cut deep. I apologized over and over, embracing, petting.

After that, when I came home, she would be happy to see me, but step away cautiously as I'd reach for her. I deserved that.

*

Still, she kept improving, more and more. The next day, she played with friends almost non-stop, and when I went to Eric and Marie's late at night, she was running, jumping, playing tug-of-war and even fetch. And around midnight, leapt over their coffee table to grab a ball.

Did we dare accept this? Was she doing it again?

*

There are measurable temperatures. The sun is hotter than a stove, ice is colder than steam. Those are facts.

But warmth, that's another thing. Shirelle is the warmest thing I've ever found. Something could be hotter, or not as hot. But nothing could be warmer.

*

One morning, I went to work to find that my supervisor was out, due to stress and a falling file cabinet spraining her wrist. Meanwhile, one of my coworkers was confined to a post-operation wheelchair. And someone had just stolen her wallet. The day before, another had broken her ankle, another had gotten a black eye (when her mom tossed her a barbecue tool and missed), and our receptionist had cut her foot open. I had smashed my head into a friend's chandelier and bled profusely.

Later that day, Shirelle's collar fell off on a walk, which had never happened before. And when we got home, she turned and bumped her head on the gate, with a frustrated whimper, that sounded like she'd been making painful mistakes like that a lot lately.

What was all this?

*

A few days later, Shirelle was at about 50 percent of her energy. Nowhere near as bad as the day she'd collapsed, but she had the pale gums again, and no appetite. She had weakened at times before, but always for a clear reason, such as swallowing a chicken breast whole. But this was worse.

I took her to the hospital. Just what I'd thought. She was bleeding again, though not as badly as before. They did a transfusion, exactly the same.

A part of me was relieved. I'd expected this all along. I didn't sense that she was going to go, just that she needed this boost, for the next stage of healing. Like two years ago, when the second operation left her stronger.

The next morning, her body was absorbing the blood well, but the tumors hadn't totally clotted. She had to stay for another transfusion. I went to see her, so she wouldn't feel so abandoned. I still wasn't feeling dread. I just wished I could take her home.

*

I had been donating blood for years, but it had never connected to my own life before. I learned that most of the blood that dogs get in hospitals comes from greyhounds who are in rehabilitation, after racing, being retrained to live in society. She would love knowing the blood she's getting comes from the fastest breed!

*

They kept her all day. That morning, our chiropractor phoned. He said he'd been doing his meditation, and Shirelle came to him in it, so he knew something was off. Was she okay?

I got to work and a coworker looked at me and said, "This is it."

"What?"

"This is the day, she's not going to make it. I can just feel it." And she said it in a way that was so normal, so like the way other people would have said, "This isn't the day," that I couldn't get angry, but insisted, "I really disagree. I've never felt as secure about her before." I walked out, pushing the scary energy off me.

It felt great to gloat later. Because, by five o'clock, I was driving home with a healthy, happy dog in my car. Both of us very pleased!

A friend had written me about a formula she'd heard of that had reduced tumors, and even eliminated some. For weeks, I had struggled, trying to contact the supplier overseas. When I finally reached him, he said they'd tried this stuff on rats, and within three or four weeks, it had eliminated 80 percent of some tumors, and then within a couple of months had made some disappear. The main side effect, he said, is that at high levels, it had caused neurotoxicity. Well, I thought, if you're gonna hurt anything in Shirelle, hurt the brain!

I offered to try it. Bothered by the communication problems, but I'd learned, especially with Shirelle, to ride it, surf it, go with the flow.

Though I did ask him to send it overnight mail.

On Tuesday the seventeenth, she was doing great. That night, the acupuncturist felt her, but only said "she's so-so." I drove her to the hospital to check her PCV, all the way there giving my biggest pep talk: "Come on girl! Clot up, we can reduce the tumors! You have new medicines, everything's going to be fine, just beat this thing. Come on girl! Come on girl!" Playing "Skylark" over and over, which seemed to charge her up.

The vet who'd worked on her the day before took her back to check her PCV. I realized who she reminded me of – a long-ago girlfriend, who'd just given birth to her second child. Had to be a good sign. She came back and gave a thumbs-up; the PCV was fine. I screamed a big "Yes!" and covered the heroic patient in kisses, and took her to get her a cheeseburger.

But when we got home, she didn't want it.

I noticed later that she was lying on the floor of my bedroom. "Of course you're a little weak from all this." I picked her up and put her on the bed. When I came back later to join her, she was looking at me knowingly, through worried caring sad eyes. I climbed in, gave her many kisses and healing rubs, and told her over and over and over.

*

In the morning, I got up while she stayed on the bed. She was to spend the day with Eric and Marie, so, a bit before I was set to leave, I lifted her off to get her legs moving. She reached the floor carefully, and instantly started panting. I wondered if I'd lifted her too quickly, or held her too tight.

I walked her around a bit. She'd stop panting, but then start again. Then I heard her drinking, and thought, good. That's what was wrong, she's just thirsty. Then after a while, I found her lying on the floor next to the empty bowl. She must have drunk a quart. And that's not a spot she ever lies in.

I looked at her gums. They weren't desperately pale, but they weren't pink bubble gum, either. Instead, in places, they had turned black.

The emergency vet took one look at her gums and said, "Uh oh." She took her back, and soon walked in with a syringe full of blood. "This was sitting in her abdomen. She's got a lot of blood there. You have to decide what you want to do. We can put her on transfusion and keep her going, but this isn't good." I told her to feed the blood until I could talk to Shirelle's doctor.

Again, paralysis in that waiting room, with my heart and life on hold. Only two questions existed. Was there a way to keep her alive, and if not, how could I fulfill my longtime promise that she would go peacefully at home, amid the sights, sounds, and smells she loved?

Eventually, I got my vet on the phone. "This might be it. Can you get away today if so?" She couldn't. She needed an assistant to do the job, and she didn't have one that day. I asked if I could be the assistant, and she said no, the dog has to be held a certain way. If you miss the vein, instead of being calm, it's burning and painful.

She called the Miracle surgeon, while I called my boss, who told me to not come to work until I was very ready.

More paralysis while calls went back and forth, messages left while someone's on hold, confusion. Then my vet called. "Here's the deal: We know she has three big tumors in her liver. We don't know what else is there. If you choose, we can open her up and look. If it's just those three tumors, we can remove them, put her back together, and she'll stop bleeding, and live weeks or more. But if there are numerous tumors, we just won't wake her up."

I thought this over. If it worked, she'd be going back to summer of 2005, where things could be good or hellish. Or we could kindly, quickly, put her down here. Or I could take her home, where she'd suffocate to death due to loss of blood.

Of course, I couldn't do the third, so I was stuck. But suddenly –

"Wait a minute! You're saying I could put her down here, or I could take her down to the hospital, where there's a small chance?" My promise had been that she'd die in her yard. But if I put her down here, she wouldn't go home, while if I took her to the surgeon, maybe she would. So the operation was the only choice.

They loaded her up with blood and fluids for the journey. The only stop I made was Eric and Marie's house. Eric came out, frightened, to give her a hug and a kiss. He stepped away from the car, and she stuck her head out with a big dumb Sylvia smile, and he burst out laughing. All felt okay. That's what she does.

They took a blood sample to cross-match, and we waited an hour to hear how it went. The vet from the previous night said that they could save a lot of trouble by checking the heart and lungs with an ultrasound, as, if they were loaded with tumors, there would be no point in operating. More waiting.

A woman whose Golden Retriever was in for cancer surgery told me her life story, about how her dog had brought her back to life at a time when she couldn't be physically touched. We hugged each other, kissing cheeks. A moment.

The results came back. Her heart and lungs were perfect. It hadn't spread. Best of all, this meant that Shirelle was in no pain, and had been in none. The liver, like the brain, has no nerve endings. So now, if the liver could be saved, she's a twelve-year-old with a raspy throat and the energy of a puppy. And a future. If.

While they set up to operate, I walked Shirelle around, and she barked at other dogs, sniffed. Life.

Throughout, I made phone calls. "It's time to pray. It's the biggest gamble ever. She wins this one, it could be years. She loses it, she's gone. It's everything."

The vet left us in a little waiting room. Constant petting and kissing. And I thought of that camping trip, when I'd thrown that tree branch down that cliff-hillside and she'd run it back up. "Girl, that's you today! You have to fight that hard!" I didn't know what she could do, but it was uphill.

They came in and gave her the pre-anesthetic, which they said might affect her a little bit, as it's a morphine derivative. It doped her up blotto. More kissing, more pep talk, more words of love.

And then they took her. And for about 25,000 hours, I tried to read a newspaper. And then the vet walked in with the saddest eyes in the world, and shook her head.

"The news isn't good."

The three large tumors they'd seen were all on one side of the liver, bleeding. But beside those, there were hundreds of smaller tumors, so many that there was more tumor than there was liver tissue. And, worst, another, larger tumor, on the other side, was meshed with the largest artery connecting the heart and abdomen. It had a big clot keeping it from simply gushing. Even if they removed the first three tumors, they could not touch that one, and by the time she recovered, it would be bleeding more. So operating wouldn't save her.

I asked, "Is it possible for you to make it good enough for me to just get her home? That's all I need. So I can let her go in her own yard tomorrow or so?" But because of that big tumor, the answer was no.

They still needed my permission. And finally I gave in.

"But can I be there? It would mean the world to me."

"Are you sure?"

"It means *the world* to me!"

She checked. Said they could wheel her into the little room. I said I didn't see any reason for all that extra work, I'd be happy to be anywhere with her. She came back and said "It's okay then, we'll just fix her up a little bit," as she was still opened up on the table.

Eventually they led me in. There she was, with a big tube down her throat, the kind that I'm sure had scratched her vocal cord two years ago. And a big diaphragmatic bag that was pumping air into her, giving her breath. They said I could hold her if I wanted.

Her torso was wrapped in a child's towel with a Disney figure's legs visible – Ariel or something. One of the staff members had brought it in for her. From somewhere inside me that could still talk, I told them about her Little Mermaid towel at home.

And as they left, I took the unconscious wrapped body into my arms and cried.

An hour, maybe more, went by. The vet came in and adjusted Shirelle slightly, and the towel fell open to show more of the figure. Tinkerbell. It never stops.

She apologized for not having cleaned the room up more. "You think I care?" But both of us knew there was nothing anyone could say that wasn't clumsy. Cautiously, we talked about pets she had, how she related to my state. And eventually, someone else came in, and while the vet held me, I held Shirelle. Her heart to mine.

I'd held dogs being put down before; normally there's a big inhale, then a very long exhale as they go. It's peaceful and beautiful. I braced myself.

I felt them put the injection into her forepaw, and I said to her the only farewell words that made sense. "Thank you."

But there was no breath. She just went, evaporated. I have never touched such peace. A sense of, "It's time. This body's done here."

And as the life went out of her, a swelling of pain seared through me, and another sentence poured out. "I will *always* love you!" And I said it over and over.

It sounded dumb to my ears. Of course I'll always love her. Why am I saying this? But I kept on.

They let me sit there with her, alone, for maybe an hour. They took her pawprint, twice, because they wrote her name on the first one but I said I'd want it without the name. I'd know whose it was. And then the doctor said it was time to get her ready to go home. She showed me the box they had for her, said it was a little small, but, "We'll curl her around and she'll be cozy," and I said, "That's perfect; that's what she does when she sleeps a lot of the time."

We talked more about something or other, and they brought her out in the box. It had a pink heart crayoned on the top, where her head lay. I opened it, and melted. She looked so sweet, so cozy, as promised, so calm. And they'd kept her in the towel.

We wheeled her out to my car, followed by the nervous eyes of pet owners in the lobby, and placed her in her back seat.

And I got in and began making awful, awful, awful phone calls.

It was her time. She went without ever becoming a feeble impaired old dog. I would have liked that, but she wouldn't. She was exhausted. I had held her, saying over and over that she needed to pick up that tree and run up the cliff, not realizing that she had been doing just that for two years. And just as was true on that mountain, there comes a time to stop. A time to rest.

And that strange thing with my vet's unavailability? I'd hoped it was the universe forcing my hand into the operation because it would save her life, but that wasn't the case. But maybe it was her, showing off again, as when she cleared our fence or scaled the mountainside. Maybe she wanted me, and all of us, to know about that liver.

It explained the Miracle. Yes, I'd pulled in every alternative medicine I could find, and *Sylvia* worked its magic. But meanwhile, the toxic blood did just what the doctors said it would do. It infected and took over her liver (though her incredible heart was way too strong for it). What the energy work, and the herbs, and the play, and all the love she got from so many people – what all of it did was to give her the strength *to live for nearly two years with a liver riddled with cancer cells!* This is impossible. This is the Miracle. This is the defiance of science, of logic, of everything. This was, and is, Shirelle.

The second-grade teacher had left me a phone message, to relate that her former student Shirel had come into her classroom that afternoon, asking if she was still in touch with that fun substitute teacher she used to have, "and his dog who has my name." And bringing her a cupcake.

Because today was Shirel's birthday.

191

I had started to change my mind about burying Shirelle in the yard, thinking that might be claustrophobic, as she didn't like sleeping with things on top of her. So maybe I should instead cremate her, and then part of her could go to the ocean, part in the mountains, part in the woods, and so on. But a friend asked if she could get me something for dinner. I hadn't eaten in 24 hours, could definitely stand something. She asked what I'd like. Some chicken maybe?

And it hit me – Yes! A roasted chicken! Shirelle never got to have chicken bones. I'd pulled so many out of her mouth. Well, now she gets them! And I've got that cheeseburger from last night. She should have that! And she should have... Forget cremation! She'll be happy in that yard, with tons of these special things!

I got home after, as I'd promised myself, buying a pack of cigarettes. It was still light. I didn't want the neighbors' kids to see the coffin, so I parked at the end of the driveway. Then, making sure I wasn't seen, I pulled it out. It was heavy and ungainly – she was much easier to carry when she had life in her – and I backed up and lost my balance, falling into a rose bush. I regained my footing, looked down, and…

The casket was festooned with pink rose petals. Exactly the same shade as the crayon heart. It was so beautiful. She was singing.

I placed the box on our tree swing, giving her the yard I couldn't earlier.

Over hours, friends showed, needing to connect. We stood near the swing, sharing favorite memories of the girl. And then the magic started again.

A breeze was blowing, lightly playing wind chimes, as I began re-assaulting my lungs. I started to tell the story about her running the branch up the mountainside, when suddenly a huge wind gusted in and blew the coffin lid off across the yard. We all turned in shock. No one doubted – she was shouting, "And I'm even stronger now!"

While guests talked or played music, I would walk away to her and look in again, and still she looked asleep – so sweet, so content. But eventually, my shock and exhaustion were too much, and I monotoned, "I don't know what anybody wants, including me, so you guys have to leave when you feel like it."

I have no memory of the rest of the night. I know I brought her inside and put the casket on four chairs, under her giant picture, and that I cried and prayed and went to sleep, but I don't remember any of it.

This had been the saddest day of my life. But it wasn't the worst. Although the week had been filled with grotesque horror, from Baghdad to Virginia, this day I'd dreaded for years had so much glory, and was filled with so many of Shirelle's amazing signature maybe-coincident miracles. Like Tinkerbell, the gust of wind, and, most beautifully, that a lovely little girl with her name was led to tell me it was her birthday.

My dog was gone. But my partner was somehow still around.

Part Six:

The Wake

Chapter Twenty-Two:
Life Itself

The next morning, I woke early. I put on a t-shirt a friend had made with a picture of Shirelle on it, under my work clothes. I saw Lydia, who knows all the houses on the block, and didn't want her to hear it from someone else.

"¿Cómo está la princesa?"

"Shirelle está…"

"¡¿En hospital?!"

"No… En el cielo."

Lágrimas.

I left work early. I bought a pickaxe for digging in the clayey yard. But heading home, I caught myself thinking, "What will she be like when I get there? Will she be sleeping, or hunting outside? Will she be in the window?"

I only now realized that I'd always done that. On a normal workday, at about 4:30, my imagination would ignite. "Oh, I'm gonna see her!" Maybe start talking to her: "I'm coming home, little girl, it won't be long!" Singing little songs. Other people look forward to going home because they get to laze, have a beer and watch mindless TV. Not me, I had never cared about relaxing. I just looked forward to seeing Shirelle. But now…

I walked up to the house. It was hitting me harder. I opened the door. And as I walked through, I saw Shirelle, but in a box.

And all at once, the deep volcano blew, exploding grief. "I Miss You! I MISS You! And I'm going to miss you for a VERY long time!"

I hadn't thought about the missing before. I'd dealt with the concept of life without her, and of her dying in my arms.

In truth, I never knew before what the word "missing" really meant. But now I did.

The ground was too hard to dig, even with a pickaxe. I moved from spot to spot, to no avail.

Marie came by, and we talked for an hour. About what had happened, and what she was. She'd written down a dream she'd had overnight.

> "Eric and I were on the road, and we got lost, driving out of the city, to a town we were told was named Buena Ser. It was like a desert but somehow with the promise of water and greenery and growth.
>
> "We came upon a little ramshackle home. Yours. We walked around back and Shirelle was there, and she followed us into the house, playing with toys, tossing them in the air and catching and shaking them with her ears up and that silly smile that always made us laugh.
>
> "I was so surprised, and I said to you, 'I thought she was sick,' and you said, 'No, she's fine,' with a small smile of profound knowing. And here was Shirelle, just bouncing around, so plump and looking so good.
>
> "We went outside, and she was chasing birds. There was a river nearby, fast flowing with rocks and willows and an arched bridge over it. And there were people on the other side walking on a path, but not in a hurry, their faces shining with contentment. One was my friend's father, who died a couple of days ago.
>
> "I wondered whether Shirelle would walk over the bridge, but I had the feeling that it was something she'd rather not do with me watching her. So I stood there in the bright sun watching this pageant, listening to the river and feeling the

desert wind moving across my face.
    "Anyway, that's about it. I just wanted to tell you that she's fine."

And in that conversation, glancing at a picture of her, Marie casually sighed out The Sentence, what I'd been trying to say for twelve years:

"It was like looking at life itself, looking at her face."

*

Within an hour, my living room was full of neighbors. Kids, teenagers, parents of assorted ages. How much that dog was loved.

People wanted to hang out, but I knew I had a huge job ahead. I sat up till 2:30 writing an email letter, telling what had happened. It ended with:

> "She is fine. It *was* Shirelle's birthday. I don't know what she was born into, but all I've felt for the last day is that it was something wonderful. Like this life was, and maybe better.
>
> "But that's her, not me. I have begun the painful job of living without this glorious being, who blew my mind daily and took care of me always. I've sent out so many pictures, I've written so much about her, and I don't think I've scratched the surface of what she was."

I then added a musical attachment, asking the reader to "play it, loud. It's a little message from the old singing group that inspired her name. Ignore the pronouns. It's from her, and from me. And it's to her, and to me, and to the world, and to all of you. And, maybe most of all, to Life Itself."

And around the world, computers sang:

201

While I'm far away from you, my baby
I know it's hard for you, my baby
Because it's hard for me, my baby
And the darkest hour is just before dawn

Life can never be exactly what we want it to be
But I can be satisfied just knowing you love me
There's one thing I want you to do, especially for me
And it's something that everybody needs

Each night before you go to bed, my baby
Whisper a little prayer for me, my baby
And tell all the stars above
This is dedicated to the one I love

*

I got up at a quarter to six, and finally found the right spot. Not such hard ground, and it would let her watch the whole yard. I worked for an hour, but still only got a few inches in. Was this going to be possible?

On my way to work, it started to rain. Good, I thought. This would soften the ground a bit, after the driest winter on record. But later, it rained harder. And harder and harder. Major streets flooded out, and I started to worry. Wendy had offered to come by and help me dig, but it could be dangerous to be pickaxing while standing in rainy mud.

I left work, and on my way home… it stopped raining.

202

Wendy brought food. We talked about *Sylvia* while we ate. And we finished, and walked outside.

And then, *just* then… the sun came out.

The ground was softer, but there was no water in the hole. We worked.

We talked about loss, about Shirelle, even laughed. Just as if she were there.

And after a couple of hours, we finished it. A really great, professional looking hole. About two and a half feet deep, more than enough.

We went inside, toasted Shirelle, and then, *right* then… the clouds suddenly broke, to rain for hours.

Once again, we stared in awe.

The pounding rain transformed the area; the world turned to mud. I'd scrape it off boots or shoes, but still it sloshed everywhere. All echoing that original order in the woods, that mud should be tracked into my house.

*

The next day, I phoned people and put together music to play at the burial.

Half of me wanted to withdraw from the world completely, while half wanted to spend all my time with friends sitting in the pain. What not one bit of me had the slightest desire to do was to phone Shirelle's loving clients. But I knew I had to, as hitting them with the news in person would be far worse. So I braced myself and called.

Most of them initially expressed only their regret for my pain. The one woman was so blacked out that I was unable to tell her for over a week, so I had to keep building up the courage to call. The most painful, however, was the young girl. Surprised to hear from me, she listened to the awful news, and said nothing. I waited, and then asked if she was all right. Still there was silence. I asked if she'd been left alone, wanting her to get her mother if so, but she misunderstood and handed her mother the phone, and walked out of the room. Her mother explained that she was dissolved in tears and couldn't manage a word.

Had I been wrong to bring Shirelle into the clinic? Would I end up doing more damage to the clients, by having brought them into my relationship, than the good she had done them? And how would I deal with the first sessions without her?

But something else was feeling off, too. As though she were complaining that this was taking too long. I could feel she needed to go under the ground soon. But, knowing she'd be buried the next morning, I curled up next to the box, to sleep one last night next to her.

*

I never slept more than a few hours these days, so woke early and began preparing for the burial. I had decided on a lot of things that were going to get buried in the hole with her: the duck from the play, one of the little red prop balls, and a lone page from the script that I'd found in a pile of scratch paper recently, where Sylvia tells Greg, "I can't believe you saved my life. I felt this connection," and he says, "I felt it too, Sylvia, you're a good girl, I'll try to give you a good home." The burger she hadn't eaten Tuesday. A cassette tape of *The Swingin' Years*. The ragged remains of her *Jurassic Park* towel. Others had brought flowers, beer, treats. Marie and Eric gave her a potato with "we love you" written on it (though they were too devastated to come). And she got the roasted chicken from Wednesday, which no one had touched, and some chocolates. The things she wasn't allowed in life.

Guests came, some crying already. I gave everyone the offer that if they wanted, they could look inside the coffin. After we talked a while, it was time. I walked out back and suddenly realized, "I've got all these people, who probably expect me to say something, and no brain to think of anything." I just thanked them, "for coming because you wanted to," and asked if anyone had anything to say. But they were shy, or polite, or just sad. So many had been saying it just didn't seem right, that she should have gone on forever.

I'd decided to wrap her in the tarp I'd made for the car. She'd always had it for safety in traveling. So why not for this trip?

I lowered her into the hole, and everybody threw something in. Not caring that it might look self-indulgent, I climbed in and kissed her nose goodbye.

And then I turned on the music. The first song was "Let's Call it a Day," by Claude Thornhill. Wistful, romantic, and so peaceful and loving.

And then, the instant that I threw the first shovel of dirt onto her, that bad feeling went away. Release. She could breathe now.

Every person there laid a somber shovel-full on. And as the last laid their dirt on her, "Yer So Bad" began, and all the mourners smiled. Truth.

We started heaping in the rest of it fast, singing along: "...the best thing I ever had..." And there was laughter and there was singing, for her.

And when all the soil was in place, I again had no idea what to do now, what to say, but then thought aloud, "Applause?" And they started in, and we all applauded her, and then we all yelled out "Good Dog!" and then I yelled louder "Bad Dog!" and others yelled that too. Joyous.

And everyone was so kind and lovely that I could almost put aside the gaping hole in me. And when they left, I left too. I had a full schedule that day. I needed it.

*

On the road, something nagged at me: Among the people there, a number were strongly religious. And while I did offer for anyone to speak, I never specifically mentioned prayer. Now if someone had asked me, "Do you really think she takes the chicken off to the next world?" I'd have said no, it's a gesture, a statement of love. For my own sake, like the music. But in so doing, did I make these lovely people feel they couldn't express their own beliefs and feelings?

I had promised to help out at a child-therapy workshop, and tried to focus there. The speaker threw a squishy ball into the audience, to demonstrate communication through playing catch. That was it: what to do with my clients. But was it just him telling me, or Shirelle too?

That night, I went home. It was raining again. Mud everywhere. I went out back to take a look, and… the grave, which had been just patted-down soil, was now covered in rose petals and bouquets. How…? Who…? And in one of the bunches was a card wrapped in plastic. I took it inside and read it. It was from neighbors from across the street, and said all they couldn't say at the burial. "Shirelle is with God now. God gave you to her and her to you, and she is in heaven now, and this is a sign of divinity in you."
More and more forgiveness.

And looking at the flowers and herbs, I heard the voice of the wistful owner in *Sylvia* looking at her picture, "She still looks absolutely gorgeous."
She always will.

206

Chapter Twenty-Three:
The Week of Weeks

I went to the nursery to get some little flowers for the grave. They were too saddened by the news to accept any pay.

*

The first day Marie and Eric came to see her resting place, I gave them the pawprint with her name, and Eric broke down crying, almost couldn't stand up.

Meanwhile, a neighbor child, who had never bought anything for anybody before, used a birthday gift card to buy me a book of pictures of dogs, to help me through this.

*

A friend, whose husband had died a few years ago, told me that she learned then why every culture has funerals: to give the grieving something to do. Because otherwise you're just stuck, feeling nothing but intolerable helplessness.

The acupuncturist's assistant called me, with kind words about the passing. Then she added that in Chinese tradition, if two beings are really close, after one dies, it stays here for 49 days. A week of weeks. In that time, that being will stay around whomever it was closest to in life, but also it will do kindnesses for those who were kind to it, and will seek revenge on those who were mean to it.

Then at the end of the seven weeks, it's time to let go. That may mean that I'm ready to let her go and she's not, so I have to push her away, or that she's ready and I'm not, and I have to be made to release her.

Sure enough, over the next few weeks, a few of our friends had boons of luck. And that dog, the one from St. Patrick's Day? For some unknown reason she went temporarily lame.

But was Shirelle really staying around me?

- The day before her burial, an old clock of my grandparents' stopped. The time didn't mean anything to me until a day later, when it was exactly the time she was buried.

- I could feel her near me in bed often. But even at work, I'd think, "Hey, there's no one here, I can invite you in now," and suddenly I'd feel her present. Against the rules!

- Then coming home one day to find a lizard in my kitchen sink. Including its tail, maybe a foot long. I couldn't figure out how it got there. It's gotta be Shirelle. I rescued it and put it outside. Go play in your yard, love.

- Or there's the time my Dispos-All broke. A repairman checked it out, no sound, no nothing. He sat down and started his paperwork, and we talked. His sister had just died. He asked if I'd ever lost anyone close to me, and I pointed out Shirelle's poster behind him. He looked, and the Dispos-All roared on – right at that moment.

The switch had been on throughout, but why did the power click on just then?

*

The Year of Deaths did not abate. A gunman opened fire in a mall near where I grew up. My boss' mother-in-law, one of my parents' closest friends, and a dear friend's mother, all went in consecutive days.

Then a coworker told me that a child she worked with had been murdered the night before. I was a wreck, too shut down from everything to empathize, or even imagine what she was feeling. I got through my clients, and when the last finished, gratefully turned on the radio and began simple paperwork.

A guest host was playing an album of Handel. Baroque music often bored me, as it always seems to be saying the same thing: "Everything makes sense, there is a Plan. And isn't that glorious." But today, I needed that.

I was alone, and so imagined asking Shirelle into the room. She came, and I thought, "You know what I haven't had in a long time, because your back legs got weak – I've always said that the nicest thing in the world is Shirelle Hugs." And she got up. But she was huge, like her size in the poster. And this giant "Tinder Box" dog put her forelegs around me and hugged me so warmly. And my heart felt all its pain, and opened, and it was all with the music.

And then the host said, "I hope you're enjoying this. I'm your host for today, Shirelle."

"WHAT?!" I called the radio station. "What is your name?" And she said "Sharon," pronounced like the prime minister.

But I'd heard what I needed to. And that helped.

*

At times I'd go into a stultified, stuck place. I stared at a dried-up lemon on a little tree that looked like a walnut. And thought, "That's my heart today."

Then the stuckness would break, and I'd get very sad. Just grieving.

Her soul was still with me. But that being, with the feet that stuck out, the ears, the eyes, the every movement. That's what was gone. And that paw. And that other paw. And that tail. And that hip-bone. And that molecule.

While I was very out of my own body, except when I would stretch and suddenly feel searing grief shoot through it, because it was all trapped in my muscles.

*

A dream. I am driving on a country road. Suddenly, I'm supposed to make a very sharp left turn, uphill on gravel. And my car can't do it. The wheels can't grab, and I slide back, toward the traffic behind me, and crash the side of my car into another car waiting to turn. It's dented, but the side of mine is smashed in.

And the dream kept recurring through the night.

*

Grief is surgically painful. But losing Shirelle was the opposite of losing a girlfriend, friendships, a job. There was nothing for me to 'figure out.' There were mistakes I regretted, but there wasn't a question of "should I get her back," or "how can I avoid this in the future?" None of the endless ruminations – "what did she mean when…" or "If I'd only…" And there was no chance of it changing.

Just a raven inside me, endlessly quoting, "Nevermore."

*

For my first sessions without Shirelle at the small clinic, I took that suggestion from the workshop by showing the clients a little red *Sylvia* ball, the one that wasn't buried, and tossing it to them. Each played catch with me, and each in a different way. But in so doing, each found a way to deal with their loss by bringing Shirelle's energy into the room.

But I still wondered if it had been pure idiocy to include her at all. And worse, had it been from selfishness? For what is worse than for a therapist to make his clients share his private emotional needs?

The answer became clear soon. At the first session after losing her, the young girl proudly proclaimed that she had built a shrine to Shirelle in her bedroom, something she'd never been able to do with the loss of her parents' marriage; she also utilized my goal of making the session about her needs by brilliantly asking to hear all the details about the burial, and not one bit about the hospital. Another client brought me food she had cooked, returning the care she'd felt from us. Another expressed surprise at the depth of his grief, realizing he had never been allowed to mourn a loss before.

And another, whose previous therapist had left without warning and died six months later, had taken a picture of Shirelle on his cell phone during a recent session. Two months from the day of Shirelle's passing, he gave me a tile with the picture painted on it, and the words of a song we had shared inscribed alongside.

As awful as the loss of Shirelle had been for all of us, my clients were each using it in their own way, to experience and express emotions they otherwise couldn't, in a space where they were met with not only acceptance, but gratitude.

It wasn't just her being a lovable mutt. Although we're talking about a therapist and a dog, these people had here found a perfect loving and supportive relationship. How many relationships that good had they been around? And, at the same time, these two loving devoted beings were focused completely on them and their needs.

In that sense, we created an ideal family. In some cases, their first.

She was still the best therapist ever.

*

I felt sick. I didn't want to eat. I walked outside and lay on the ground at the grave, and fell asleep. It was lovely to lie there, feel the earth, look at the pretty herbs and flowers, and have a little Shirelle time. I needed that as much as anything physical.

*

And eventually the forty-nine days passed, and, as predicted, it felt like Shirelle wasn't standing around me anymore.

Instead, she'd become part of the air, everywhere. While it used to feel like someone might jump on me.

I wasn't free of the grief at all. It was just a different sadness. And a harbinger of the process yet to come.

Chapter Twenty-Four:
The Voice

Two months after Shirelle, my client who'd suffered the blackouts died, having been denied a liver transplant. Her mother phoned me with the news, unable to access her grief, but speaking of the glory and peace her deep faith asserted her daughter had found. My mind fixed on the memory of her petting Shirelle, both staring at me, seeming to want to tell me something very important.

A thought came to me, and I wanted to tell the mother about it, but hesitated, afraid to offend her beliefs. But then, remembering the open spirit her equally devout daughter had shown, I dared:

"I have this image. When the life went out of her body, she, as we always hear, started walking down a dark tunnel, toward a distant light. But the tunnel is long, and she's confused. Till a floppy-eared dog walks up to her and says, 'I knew you'd be coming. I had to get here first so I could show you the way to go.' And leads her into the light."

She broke down in sobs, and whispered, "Thank you! That's exactly right. Shirelle's with Jesus; she's there to help her!"

Shirelle continued to come up in sessions at least once a week. One client announced that his daughter was pregnant, and might name the baby Shirelle (not in honor of the dog, but just because she'd heard the name mentioned and liked it). Another client was talking about meaning in life, and we wondered whether Shirelle had felt meaning in hers. We left it open, but later, he phoned me. "I know she was aware of her own meaning," he said. "I know there was something grander about her, because of the way she was with me. She always knew what was going on with me, and it wasn't sight or smell. It was her."

*

After the loss of my client, the deaths slowed down to about one every two weeks.

- A friend writing a play about John Lennon told me that that John had come to him in a dream, saying, "You need to talk to Doug." In May, right after Shirelle, and just before he learned that his mother was dying of cancer.

- Another friend's dog fell into a deep hole, and then suffered lots of pain. Turned out it wasn't from the fall; he was riddled with cancer and had to be put down.

- And then in late August, my brother's dog developed shakes, and her eyes started rolling back in her head. Brain tumors. Also put down.

So here I was yet again, saying I knew Shirelle'd be there as an escort to Heaven for her playmate and cousin. And as Stu and I traded thoughts on such things, a beautiful image came to me: That when it comes my time, and I find myself in that long dark tunnel, St. Peter's gates will be overtaken. Not by demons breaking in – it'll be this long tall Knucklehead, pulling herself up and bounding over them, breaking out of Paradise. To tackle me.

*

A friend told me this rash of deaths was about a Mars-Pluto conflict, and that it would last through 2007. And in truth, it did abate early in '08.

But for now, although the losses continued, I kept thinking I would start to feel better. But the opposite happened. Instead of the sadness dissipating, I was pulled deeper, into a darker place. A dank hell, far beneath grief's purity.

It began with another dream: Shirelle comes up out of the grave, into my living room, slightly deteriorated, but alive. I'm so happy, telling everyone about it.
I woke up, jolted. But instead of joy, I was filled with bitter anger.
No idea why.

And another: A former client of mine comes to my clinic, and one part of my job is that I have to put him down, like an animal. I am very uncomfortable with having to do this. But they say it will be easy, because he has such a small heart.
This dream recurred over a few nights, but I'd always forget it when I'd awaken.
Then one day, I semi-woke, and struggled with this quandary, until it hit me that it was a dream. Not that I remembered that we didn't poison our clients; it was that this guy was too old to be at this clinic, so it couldn't be real!
I laughed at myself and lay back down to return to sleep. But just then a horrible wave came over me. And I saw them putting the anesthetic into Shirelle, seeing it go in, watching them lead her out of the room. And I felt, more than I had at the actual time, my fear of what was coming. And a horror at sending her into surgery as her last consciousness. On the cold concrete floor of the hospital – the place she most feared.
And my heart began to throb in pain.

The next day, I had to help hospitalize a schizophrenic client. On realizing he was about to be strapped down, an awful frightened smile came onto his face, as he stepped backwards begging "no, no." Absolute fear. Even worse to see because of the compliance of his cheerful expression while feeling utter betrayal.
I shivered deeply. He was Shirelle, so sweet in the hospital. The horror.

A few days later, I got food poisoning. While feeling the chill symptom, I suddenly relived driving Shirelle to the hospital. The fear, hope, deep dread.

It was clear where all this was going. And sure enough, a few nights later, I bolted awake in terror, living the euthanasia.

As if I could experience her awareness of what was going on. That the man she most trusted handed her over to them. That *he* abandoned her to be cut up. That *he* said "yes." That *he* threw her away. That *he* held her still while they slipped a needle into her veins and injected her with poison to kill her.

Did she know all that, but not know why? How must that betrayal have felt?

And my mind swung to the party, the dog biting Shirelle. I became consumed by it. The bite on the face. Her frantic terror that night. The wound that never healed.

Guilt screamed around me. For all my failures – the bad leash, her feet slipping out, the open door at that party, throwing her as a puppy, not being there when she needed me. And why didn't I think to take a day off work to pursue other healers, or just to be with her? For all my talk of love, she must have always felt like an afterthought.

But what consumed me even more was the searing memory of all her fear. She hadn't gone through a lot of pain. But so much fear. The kindest soul, deserving nothing but love, filled with terror on terror on terror.

I was getting my old wish, to know Shirelle's heart. Which meant feeling all the worst she had felt. And it led me to the only possible conclusion – that, yet again, I had been a failure. I had failed to free her last days, weeks, from fear and pain and abandonment. Her final experience on earth was betrayal and horror. She didn't know my love at all, just my rejection and neglect.

And I begged to her, "Shirelle, can you tell me you're okay?"
And heard nothing.

I was empty, except for self-loathing beyond regret. I went though the motions of the day, but for no reason.

That night, I hoped for sleep, while dreading my dreams.

But hours later, as I lay in the dark, a voice came to me. A voice so disembodied as to have no sound, just existence. "You're right. You're right about the fear. It was horrible. But the fear goes when you die.

"I'm not afraid anymore. I know you always loved and cared for me, as much as you could. And it's so kind that you would feel my terrible fear. But the fear has gone. And I'm all right."

Was that just a self-healing part of me talking? Or was it really her? No way to say. But just seeing the possibility was enough to free me from the horror of her last breaths, and send my mind forward.

To the next moment.

To question…

Holding her as her life left her body. Even then, I'd wondered why the words "I Will Always Love You" were coming out of my mouth. Some Dolly Parton or Whitney Houston thing? It seemed so odd: Of course I would always love her. There was no reason for me to say it.

But… *Was* it me saying it?

Or could it have been… *Shirelle's voice?* Coming through me? *To* me?

I hadn't felt the breath of release I'd expected as her spirit passed, or the slam of energy rushing through me others described. But we were so close – could she have taken over my voice, with me unable to tell the difference?

217

It was the only explanation. But still, it was hard for me to accept. All those mistakes, those remorses – I hadn't kept her safe or alive, I'd broken my promise to take her home, even the cancer might have been my fault...

Could she, in her instant of dying, have still loved me that much?
And if so, could I let that enormity in?

Chapter Twenty-Five:
Putting It Together

A couple of months had gone by. I was slowly healing.

I sat in a session. A child was having problems at school, and her parents were distraught. They had done everything they could to raise their daughter right, but were now begging me for help. We got to talking about their pasts, childhoods of poverty and fear in an unwelcoming land. They had come so far, achieved so much. "But you know, all this money, it means nothing to me," the father confided. "The only thing that makes a man a success is if he can give his kid what he didn't have."

That's a tall order. What if one's childhood were comparatively stable? What if there's nothing you could ever give anyone that you didn't already have? Then you can't ever become a success?

We kept talking, and the mother expressed her horror at their daughter refusing to do her homework, and using language to Mom she'd be ashamed to repeat. "Have you ever heard of a child talking that way to their parent? In my home, a child never dared be so rude, so angry."

I smiled and nodded. I knew that, at some point, every youngster deals their parents such fury, such rudeness, whether they notice it or not. But I also sympathized with the mother, and so thought about how to undo this problem, and help these good people out.

And then, the colors of the room started to fade. I began to lose my breath.

Suddenly, the pieces of a puzzle I'd struggled with for years started coming together.

This whole discussion about success and failure meant these parents were basing their self-worth on their kid. And that couldn't happen unless they were in a mindset at least similar to my Language of Shame. And their daughter was so angry because she was in it too – in it because her parents were in it. How could we break this vicious cycle? Is it possible?

Could a member of such a family be freed from this Language?

I had to shut my eyes. I started talking without thinking, the thoughts seeming to skip my brain, wafting out of my mouth:

"Your daughter is suffering from Shame. You need to start building other ways for her to think."

"And how do we do that?"

"I don't... I'm sorry but I..."

An image came before me. A table leg, a rug, cleaning powder. And an angry first bark.

"You need to honor and love her voice. Even when you are disciplining her, criticizing her."

Shirelle's first bark. My swoon at that pathetic roar. Her anger was greeted with acceptance and love. Affection pouring onto her.

It wasn't an unexplained miracle that Shirelle had lived without Shame. It was because of my unthinking acceptance of, and ability to adore, her voice. So easy for me then, and such a key. That little moment was everything.

"But won't that teach her to misbehave, to disrespect?"

"No. It will..." A head lying on my heart. A noble beast high on a rock. "It will enable her to be loving and strong."

"But it's not possible for a person to live without Shame, is it?"

And at that moment, I knew I'd been there. Without even realizing it. In the searing purity of grief after I'd lost Shirelle, I had had no intelligence, no mental workings – and thereby no Shame – to get in the way of the pain. Ruminations are all about Shame. And life without Shame means pure joy, and pure suffering.

"Not completely, but one can have moments."

"But how do we know when to do that? How do we know how to do it right?"

Images flying past me. Throwing her across the yard, pushing her down from the fence, the squirt bottle in the face. "You won't know. You'll make mistakes. Hundreds. But if you always come from that respect, that love of her voice, you'll…"

"We'll spoil her."

I smiled. Where had I heard that word before? "No, she'll spoil you. And when you need it most, she will have the strength and love to understand and forgive everything you've ever done."

As my angel had to me.

My heart was beating so loud in my chest, I feared they could hear it.

"But it sounds like you're saying to raise her very differently from the way we were raised. To go against our traditions. This is what we were afraid a therapist would…"

"I'm just saying what you said to me. That the only true success is when you give something you didn't have yourself."

They thought about what I said. And so did I, but in a very different way.

It was so crazy, wasn't it? I had freed her to live her life, but I had meanwhile held fast to my own Shame. Shackling myself to my own idiocy, sabotaging every gift I'd ever had that gave me power, while waiting for outside validation to make me feel powerful. I not only allowed but relished the joy she lived, while redefining my every success into failure.

I looked up at the couple's eyes, but couldn't help the curious smile on my face. The father studied me skeptically. "And have you been such a success, sir?"

Eyes, grateful loving eyes, gazing up at me from rugs, warning me with sad knowing from a bed. A voice coming to me in my darkest night.

My mouth said, "Still trying." But inside, I shyly smiled, "Maybe now."

*

So I'd been wrong all those years. I'd had success, beautifully, but never seen it as my own. I could have validated myself any time, but didn't have the self-validation to know it. Shirelle was her own being, but also my greatest achievement.

And so, a new journey arose. To discover what exists on the other side of this fence I was just learning to clear. To move forward, without these brakes of Shame. Like recovering from any other addiction, it's work, and always will be. I'll never be free from its pull. But it will get easier, if I can just remember to pay attention.

If I should find career success, maybe I'd be able to acknowledge it unlike before, and skip the self-sabotage; and if the right romance should step into my life, maybe I'd now be able to follow Nat Cole's dictate – just to love and be loved in return.

And if I mess up, and I let Shame in again, maybe that sweet forgiving angel will suddenly turn into a raging attack-dog, and take a good bite out of it.

And give me yet more reason for gratitude.

*

222

I knew what picture I'd use for that year's Christmas card, which would also be an announcement of her passing. It had always been my favorite of her – crouched in grass, stalking me, about to pounce. But it didn't seem enough for this weighty occasion.

I found some tiny heart charms that could be put on thin golden chains, and attached one to each card. Sort of a miniature of what the Wizard gave the Tin Man. It made each a statement of her, though having to individually craft them just about left me blind.

It worked. People were touched, felt a bit of what I felt every time I thought of her. No longer guilt or remorse, just… look at that beautiful heart.

One couple wrote me that they had removed the heart from their card and hung it as a keepsake ornament, to remember her.

It would always be the tiniest thing on that tree. That perfect little heart, dangling in the air, laced with gold.

*

All is beautiful. I look around and let it in. A cool morning, the air not too humid or too dry, just a few clouds in the hazed blue. I sniff the air. The suburbs smell of honeysuckle and roses and fertilizer, while the parks and streets exude exhaust and barbecues and sweat. I listen. Strangers' laughter mixes with bird songs and barks and motorcycle engines. It's a perfect day for hiking or working outdoors, but my loyalty and an urge for play conspire to get me onto the artificial construct of a tennis court for my regular Sunday morning match, and get my mind off the date I have planned that night.

As always, I ask Barry about his beautiful wife and their young daughter. Barry married late in life, and has always been unfailingly grateful for both. But today, he looks at me with a studying wince. "You know," he begins, "I've always been happy with Henriette, and of course I'm thrilled to have little Sarah. But this morning I realized, more than I ever had before, how amazing it is to have this family. Really, it truly is the best thing ever."

I look to his eyes. No, he didn't make that word choice with any awareness of what it would mean to me.

And as such, I feel a promise, a belief in what might one day remake me whole.

"It must be," I smile, serve with all my strength, and lunge to chase the speeding returning ball.

Afterword:
Owed to Joy

We can never be dogs. We can't return to Eden and find the purity and innocence we've lost. Those who try to prove they have, from "straight passion" sorts like Sid Vicious and John Belushi, to "cleansed soul" types like Jim Bakker and Ted Haggart, meet the inevitable desserts of their core dishonesty.

But we can aim. We can think on Adam and Eve, or look into the eyes of a child, or watch an animal, and be reminded of what total integrity looks like. While our brains will always get in the way of our achieving it, these role models can remind us of what we lack – giving us the one necessary ingredient for the human race to evolve yet higher: Humility.

As we laugh at a dog kicking dirt onto her poop, we can see the absurdity of our trashing the planet but keeping poisons out of sight. When dogs run instinctively to a fight they have no part in, we can be reminded of our love of war. And, when one special dog walks away from such fights, pleasing her owner no end, we can ponder how a Creator might look at us.

In her later years, I saw nothing in her but love (with occasional fear). She barked at passing dogs, out of love. She loved the squirrels she tried to kill. She loved sleeping and waking. She loved living, and, if my sense was right, she loved death and burial. Love had become her essence, her core. Her Language.

Every major religion eventually aspires to this. The Imams preach it, the Rabbis study it, the Dalai Lama talks of little else. And Jesus, to the end, insisted it was the way.

I will never be Shirelle. Cursed by intelligence and self-awareness, I cannot. But this book is a record of my aim, and of what I was taught, by superhuman perfection.

And a howl at the moon... that the melody, of the song she was, might somehow linger on.

The Great Teachings

This book holds hundreds of the lessons I learned from, or through, Shirelle. But a few of them, the hardest to achieve, are worth another glance.

1.   Teaching limits with love and acceptance may be the single greatest gift one can give a dog, or a child. They are listening, always.

2.   Joy awaits when we're mired in misery, and is the only thing that can save us.

3.   A connection can become so deep that one feels the other's happiness more deeply than either feels their own.

4.   Speak depth through the heart, not the brain.

5.   Beauty comes from relaxed confidence, a glowing heart, and acting fully.

6.   Follow your instinct, your inner voice. If you listen to it correctly, it will not steer you wrong.

7.   Sometimes we're just not enough.

8.   The greatest warriors win, not by fighting, but by ending the fight.

9.   Keep your pleasure receptors open, and act accordingly.

10. Denying your shadow self can work against you. Be kind, but stay aware of your own feelings without judgment.

11. Initiate Play.

12. There are voices out there you haven't heard. But you can, if you try.

13. Never choose ignorance, or, worse, express pride in it.

14. You can learn a lot about yourself, and improve your life, by focusing on something you fully love.

15. There is a Language of Shame – a mentality of unconscious living in the fear, avoidance, and sureness of Shame, that extends past awareness, down generations of families, and beyond our conscious speech and acts – which, if unchecked, can prevent fullness and meaning in life.

16. Every millisecond is new. Everything is rebirth.

17. Don't lose hope; stay grateful. Things might be for the best.

18. If you find something you truly care about, do all you can for it; you'll create an energy to allow amazing things to occur.

19. Miracles happen.

20. While we work to care for someone, we may not realize how much they're taking care of us at the same time.

21. The meaning of life is Passion. Life without Passion is meaningless. The quality that makes great art is Passion. But you can't figure out your Passion. You come across it or it finds you.

22. Love Thoughtlessly.

23. Giving someone something you never had yourself is a profound success.

24. You can't get Validation from others, and knowing so is its own freedom. But Validation is achievable, from realization of one's own worth.

25. There Are Such Things. Pay Attention.